Interim

Essays & Mediations

HAGIOS
PRESS

Interim

Essays & Mediations

Patrick Friesen

For Trisha,
Best Wishes t
a good year —
Patrick Frie

HAGIOS PRESS
Box 33024 Cathedral PO
Regina SK   S4T 7X2

Library and Archives Canada Cataloguing in Publication

Friesen, Patrick, 1946-
    Interim : essays & mediations / Patrick Friesen.

ISBN 0-9739727-0-X

    I. Title.

PS8561.R496Z469 2006   C814'.54   C2006-901930-4

Edited by Allan Safarik.
Designed and typeset by Donald Ward.
Cover concept by Marijke Friesen.
Cover photo by Margaret Sawatzky Friesen.
Cover design by Yves Noblet.
Set in Sabon.
Printed and bound in Canada at Houghton Boston Printers &
Lithographers, Saskatoon.

The publishers gratefully acknowledge the assistance of the
Saskatchewan Arts Board, The Canada Council for the Arts,
and the Cultural Industries Development Fund (Saskatchewan
Department of Culture, Youth & Recreation) in the production of
this book.

In memory of, and gratitude for,
Melvin C. Toews and Victor S. Cowie,
teachers.

Contents

Introduction

AT FORTY I BEGAN TO REALIZE I HAD A HISTORY. I sensed a shadow just behind me; I'd glance over my shoulder as if I might see it out of the corner of my eye. While still moving forward, I now had a past that had solidified. Well, not solidified, but a presence for sure. Fact and memory and story woven into a shadow. There was the human existing in the moving present, part fact, apparently, and already part memory, and the reconfiguration of memory, and there was another human, much more deeply woven into story. Was the shadow controlling me, or was I shaping the shadow? It was a strange feeling. It was a weight. To change the metaphor, it was a cloak I didn't want thrown across my shoulders, but which I nevertheless dragged along behind me.

Part of this book is a recognition of that history, a history that is both apart from, and a part of, me; a history of how the adult learns to misplace what's true, and sometimes finds a way back. Finding some of these pieces made me curious. Where had some particular idea come from, where had the tone in another piece come from, or gone to? Contradictions everywhere but, then, contradictions are not a problem; the elimination of them can be.

I tried my hand at literary criticism, something I was never very interested in, nor particularly good at, but I felt I needed to give it a try. Usually it became something different in the writing of it. When one enters writing it can go anywhere. There were also pieces on poetry and its process. Thinking in one way about another way of thinking. Strange, really.

I wrote pieces on my past, on where I came from on earth; essays related to that in various ways. In the last few years, I have found myself writing fairly short prose meditations that are "takes" on small obsessions, observations, on perspectives that are my thinking at that particular moment. Sometimes they are pieces I write at night when I can't sleep because my mind is anxious or teeming with oddities and flashes, simple ideas pursued for a short distance. These are my favourite pieces.

There are moments and intervals; there are months and years and pauses. Thinking shifts, mood and conditions alter, conditions like aging, experience, learning and, just as important, unlearning in order to begin again. The body, including the brain, changes. There isn't any real progress in the way we usually think of that word; there are only different depths of both wisdom and ignorance. And often what seemed to me wisdom ends up ignorance, and the other way around. And there is an on-going curiosity, and a wonder in being alive in the body on earth.

There are a few rants; there's a time for a rant, for anger, though today's certainty is tomorrow's doubt, and one should always take an occasional glance in the mirror during a rant. It's rarely the content of a rant that I now wonder about. That comes and goes. It's the tone that makes me wonder, sometimes with chagrin, sometimes amusement or approval, but always without regret.

I also wrote a few pieces in European cities, about aspects of these cities. I find an affinity for old cultures that seem to touch, one way or another, who I am, even if they're simply background for immediate events.

Several pieces were written out, but intended as talks or panel presentations. I think better with my fingers at the keyboard than on my feet in public. That feels like a personal loss sometimes, a loss that comes from depending on the written word too much.

There are some things I see running through the collection as a whole. There is a circling around themes like loss and longing, around particular phrases, images. Trying for other angles, an overlapping of phrases, sentences, ideas, essays; a process of layering and repetition as a rhythmical device to drive thinking. Returning

Interim: Essays & Mediations

to places, often years later, that I still don't fully inhabit. It's strange how a word, or phrase, can occupy one. Usually the word moves to the periphery, after some exploration; others stay for the long term, for life. It could be sleepy habit, or it might be something I never reach the end of. And, most likely, I never inhabit any place permanently.

I recognize my dislike of ideology of any kind. It has to do with who I am. Partly this has to do with the cultural, religious milieu I grew up in. Mennonites called themselves non-resistant, but this, in itself, became a resistance to authority which expects compliance. Ironically, I found myself in resistance to their take on religion, another authority. I learned that people want to shape you into someone other than who you are, and if you're not awake you might accept their definition of you. Where I come from mixed with my personality; it gets tricky.

There are times to say no and times to say yes, and sometimes they mean each other. There are times for anger, times for joy. I give away my familiarity with Ecclesiastes, that great book. The Bible was an important influence in numerous ways, many of them not formally religious. Imagery, sound, rhythms. King James English was the conduit of something that began in another place at another time. The conduit was probably as important as the content for me.

So the English language, though of the past, entered my world in a powerful way very early. My first, and daily, language of speech at home was an unwritten dialect, Low German. High German was a school subject and heard once a month in church sermons. It was not as immediate to me as Low German or English, which I had learned well by the time I was four or five, though with a bit of an accent. My mother taught me to read English. English was my first written language.

There are times to sustain a process of thinking at some length. There are times to be fragmentary and let the fragments hold whatever truth they seemed to have at the time they were momentarily almost grasped. To develop fragments, often, is to write in stone what is only true in water. Some thinking does not need development, only expression. Face it, most thinking doesn't need to be expressed at all. What really needs to be said? There is so much to unlearn. So, why this need to write?

Primarily, for me, it's a way of working something through, praying sometimes. Bridging. It's very personal in impulse. I can't speak for anyone but myself. If I do that well, if I am truly in my self, I've done a lot, as much as I can expect. Particularly in poetry there is a quickness and immediacy I value. Something that doesn't want to be nailed down; it wants to move and disappear.

Mostly I've written poetry, drama, and text for music in one form or another. I've written prose most of my life as well, but the bulk of it wasn't sent out to be published. I often write prose non-fiction to clarify my thinking, to myself, in another way. Drama has, occasionally, been another way of necessary thinking for me. But I always return to the poetic, a process I trust most fully.

Some of the prose was published. Included here are a few of those early essays, found and gathered. I have edited, to varying degrees, several of these essays. This is primarily intended for greater clarity of punctuation and, occasionally, better word choices, but that is a tricky endeavour, with the inevitable shifts in time. I stayed as close as possible to the initial intentions and meanings. The pieces range over a quarter of a century. They are set up roughly in chronological order, but only roughly. Almost exclusively, though, the oldest essays exist within the first nine.

There were other pieces, but I've never kept an accurate record of where things were published, or when, and some that I found in old folders were incomplete and not worth completing. Some of the journals other essays appeared in have vanished from my shelves, probably in the course of moving. A natural culling. I've gone through intentional spasms of culling as well. I used to burn all unpublished works on New Year's Eve. Too much stuff, too much dust. Still, while the work that's disappeared is as important to me as what remains, what's left is part of the shadow, a small shadow I didn't know I was shaping. And still am. Remembering and writing it down, a small death each time. One human life among the billions of lives of endless species, one man's thinking in print; constantly pulling the rug out from under his own feet.

Interim: Essays & Mediations

Silence

_____

ON HIS OWN, LET'S SAY HOEING IN THE GARDEN just as light was fading, or measuring plywood in the basement, my father sometimes whistled. He was good. I never could get it right. Or, he might hum to himself, a hymn usually. Often, though, he was silent as he went about his work. Now, when I think back to my youth, I realize that in his silence he was palpably present. I knew, always, when he was in the house. He was not absent.

I wondered once why mother's books were often underneath the sofa cushions. She told me that when she and father were first married she was reading a novel one evening. After a while she couldn't help but notice that he was pacing in the room. She asked him what the problem was. He replied, "you're not here." After that, she said, although he didn't ask her to stop reading, in fact he took pride in finding used books for her to read, she read only when he was out of the house or having his Sunday afternoon nap. When she saw him round the corner, returning from work, she'd slide the book under the cushion.

He didn't mind her reading, but he was nervous, restless, when she read while he was around. What does this say about silence, about presence and absence? He was not a well-educated man, and English was his second language. So, did he feel left out of the world of the reader's imagination? Or did he want his wife and lover to be present with him just as he was present with her? Could she ever be as present as he was? She loved entering her imagination. He loved earth. A carpenter and gardener; hammers, potatoes and gladiolus.

What I remember is this: mother reading, looking lost in a calm way, father's striding figure, physically centred, at peace with that. Yet, unable to cross over to the world of the reader.

Father talked on social occasions, but not much. More than once I marvelled at how quiet it was when he and his brothers visited. Not many words. A lot of subtle physical gestures though. I got to know his physical movements; how he crossed his legs when he sat, how his working man's fingers played intricate woven games, how he tilted his head, how he touched things. Physical talk. Never long stories or anecdotes. Humour was succinct, brief and, therefore, more a wry resonance than a punch line.

All three of the brothers, when in agreement or simply under-standing something or encouraging the other to continue, drew air in across lips and teeth in a kind of whispering, almost hissing, assent. That small, sibilant intake of air was my father listening, interacting. Almost silent, but fully there.

My father-in-law was of the same generation as my father. Also raised on a farm. In his retirement he returned to a gentleman's farm and horses. This was a deep love. My daughter would stay on the farm some summers, as long as a month sometimes. I ob-served once as Grandpa G. moved among three horses tethered near the barn, currying them. My daughter watched with com-plete attention. He wasn't saying much, and what he was saying had almost nothing to do with instructions. He spoke nonsense, gently, to the horses as he moved easily among them, lifting a leg to check a hoof, patting one on the rump, and so on. She watched and learned.

Silence is not always an absence, but silent action is often how men teach. Perhaps it was that generation of men. Silence, in fact, is necessary to be a human, fully. To be in a body. To know that body, to know other bodies, to know how bodies communicate. Things happen in silence.

I recall reading an interview with the cellist Mstislav Rostropo-vich in which he spoke of Dmitri Shostakovich. Sometimes, he said, Shostakovich would phone him and tell him, urgently, to come over. Rostropovich would arrive and take a seat near Shostakovich. For half an hour there was silence. Then Shostakovich said, "that's good, thank you, now you can go." He needed not only silence but silence with another human. A shared silence. He did this with other people as well. It probably said something about the USSR at the time, but it was also about Shostakovich, silence and human physical presence.

My father's father, too, was a silent man. So, perhaps, a family trait as much as a fact of those generations of men. I used to bike to his farm, exploring in the bush, finding clearings with the bones of long-dead horses and cattle, trying to catch fish in a small creek. I wouldn't see my grandfather all day. When I ran into him there was no greeting, no words at all. A nod of recognition, a smile of surprise. Later, an offer of lemonade. Laughter at how clumsily I forked hay into a loft. But I knew the man was there. Even hidden in the bush, I somehow knew where he was in relation to me. So, probably he, too, knew where I was.

Another silence in my father. I'd heard he loved to play guitar and sing Wilf Carter songs when he was young. He may well have yodelled as well. Once he chose to devote his life to his specific spiritual beliefs, he stopped playing and singing this kind of music. He'd still sing hymns, whistle them, but no more "worldly" music, nothing that trivial, nothing secular. What kind of silence was that? A man rooted in his physicality on earth silencing a part of the voice he had enjoyed.

Once you've learned song, once you've learned words, silence is different. It can be a withholding, a restraint. Earlier, was it an incapacity?

You can hide behind, within, words.

You can release words, doing your best to say what you think, what you mean. But the words, in their impressions, their approximations, may be heard to say something other than what is meant. Now you need to explain, or reword, or if they have a finality to them and can't be retrieved, you need to follow them, back them up, or change your thinking, to live them.

A man's silence often isn't silence, but wordlessness. There can be sounds; intakes of breath, whistles, grunts, the click of the tongue.

You give yourself away with words. If you're silent, people fill in, with imagination, with assumptions, what you are. You may be over-estimated, given strength and thoughts you may not have. Power in withholding.

With the silence, after words, do we need to fill it? Does it ask to be filled as nature abhors a vacuum? Was the entry of language into the world the snake in the garden?

Words emerge, vanish; a person vanishes, leaving behind the sutures that knit the air where the person was.

To paraphrase Wittgenstein, one must be silent about what one cannot speak about. If it cannot be adequately spoken one must be still. On one level it makes sense. If you can't say it, don't. I think my father and his brothers believed this. Words are not to be wasted.

However, this doesn't take into consideration the music of language, the sounds of it. It doesn't accommodate the approximateness of human thought and expression. It doesn't recognize the comfort of sound between two or more people. I include the music of sounds between words. The breathing, the small sounds of agreement or disagreement or simply acknowledgement that something has been heard.

It brings me to poetry, that inadequate expression of human experience, of human thinking. It brings me to song. Those fine gradations between singing and whistling, between words and physical gestures. The silences that speak, and those that withhold. The silences that are enforced.

The human body fully present on earth, on its way into earth. Part of this physical presence is air moving in and out of lungs, passing by vocal cords. Tongue, teeth and lips that can shape the air. How do we do it? How do we remain in our bodies, not too abstracted into language? How do we enliven the body with the sound of words?

I Could Have Been Born in Spain

1. I WAS BORN INTO THIS. I could have been born in Spain. Barcelona maybe, or Seville. If the winds had shifted that night. Or Ireland. When I was eleven or twelve I thought I must have been an Irish foundling. I had the name.

Mother told stories of gypsies who traveled through Altona in small caravans each year. At night she sang me to sleep with Irish ballads. She named me.

Father's mother died when he was four. He lost the sight of his right eye before he was ten. Father used to like Wilf Carter. I think he even owned a guitar. He stopped singing that kind of music when he was saved.

2. IT WAS IN A FIELD, TREES NEARBY and, behind them, you could hear a small river. It was a Sunday school picnic. Mother stood at a long table with other women. They were making Klik sandwiches and potato salad. They were talking in Low German. Stories of the week, humorous things they had seen or done. Some talked more than others. Mrs. P. D. Friesen had the greatest laugh I'd ever heard; it was completely uninhibited.

I stood beside mother. If only I hadn't had to wear that stiff white shirt, everything would have been fine. A blue sky, soft breeze and all that familiar talk. I was drinking a glass of lemon-lime Kool-Aid.

Men stood a little way off, at the edge of the trees. A few leaned against willows. Most stood erect, arms across their chests. They wore white shirts with sleeves rolled up. I couldn't hear what they were talking about.

It was funny how the men stood side by side talking straight ahead. They talked face-to-face during the week. The women were usually in groups. Around tables, around bowls, around the house.

3. I SQUIRMED IN THE PEW, wishing to be outdoors. I learned subversion here.

With friends, I whispered behind my hand, or ducked my head behind the pew, suppressing laughter. We made sly comments about ministers and many-armed song leaders. We jeered at strange flowered hats and drab brown or black clothes.

Sometimes everyone stood to sing. Occasionally this was deeply moving. Sometimes everyone got down and kneeled to pray. Once, I remember, someone a few rows away broke wind. Whoever it was, this person was trying to keep it in, you could tell, because what emerged was a long, pinched squeal.

I loved the maps at the back of the Bible. I spent many Sunday mornings poring over the names and shapes and colours of these maps. I saw where Jesus walked on water, where Mary Magdalen found the open tomb. I loved the name Samaria.

When the words in the air weren't dead, I sometimes heard piety, sometimes anger that judges and seeks vengeance on all unbelievers. I often heard the word love, but it never felt like love. I wondered why, because outside of church love was much easier to find. And so was joy.

I loved The *Revelation* of John of Patmos. I loved the candles and horses, the river and the trumpets. I loved the whore of Babylon arrayed in purple and scarlet. She had to be magnificent. I thought she was voluptuous and beyond yes and no. The book was never allegory for me; it was all the magnificent truth of image and symbol. It turned out I loved the very things that were being condemned.

I liked to think I would be safe at the end of the world. I knew there was another life to be lived. The kingdom was within each of us. Then, when I learned heaven was outside someplace, and I, and most other people, had no right to claim it, *Revelation* became frightening. It was a threat, a punishment. *Revelation* wanted to destroy the world. There was a self-righteous lust to be rid of the world.

Revival meetings were my blast furnaces. Here I learned to conceal emotions. I learned to play tough. I remember the choreography. The frightening sermon, the tear-jerking hymns, altar call, the men watching from the back of the church, or from the platform in front, watching for signs of personal turmoil, watching, then moving toward some troubled person, arm around their shoulder, whispering into that torment, cajoling, pushing.

I think most gave in out of fear. Some grew hard. Or, you became sly; skipping, stumbling, lying, cursing, laughing toward a distant day of freedom.

Those voodoo evenings of spiritual violence. No matter what choices were made, how many survived with their spirits full and rejoicing?

4. WHEN I WAS YOUNG, I loved the stories missionaries brought back with them. I soon realized that, although I enjoyed the stories, I didn't like what the missionaries were doing to the people they went to live with.

It seemed presumptuous to intrude on people in other countries and manipulate them to abandon their spiritual beliefs and cultures and adopt the new sanctified one. As if only people who called themselves Christian (who often rejected other branches of Christianity) had a monopoly on wisdom, on the spiritual reality of existence.

Like other cause-obsessed people, it seemed missionaries, generally, projected onto others the shadows they could not accept in themselves. So, they went to war against a mirror. We, afraid of our own shadows, urged them on.

Today I think about Africans and South Americans who can't find a rightful place in their Christian societies, who don't know anymore what they are, as the new society rejects them, and they can no longer return to what they once were.

The missionaries, compared to the oilmen and the military, were the soft armies. Wearing their pith helmets and white shirts. They brought the Word, as they understood it, and this Word fell like a hammer on delicate old worlds.

5. WHEN FATHER WAS GOING BLIND, with bandages on his good eye, he would identify birds I couldn't even hear. He named them as they flew over or hopped among the tomatoes. I thought the birds were

in his head; his head an open field where robins tugged at worms and sparrows fell.

Father shot left-handed because of his blind eye. It was confusing, at first, when he tried to teach me to hunt. I would line up my shot but, automatically, close my right eye, as if I was aiming left. I learned to shoot well. Father and I shooting in different directions.

I shot right-handed in hockey, too. I was proud of this because Gordie Howe was a right-hander. I think the Rocket was as well, but I had learned to fear him.

Father let me listen to the first two periods of hockey on Saturday night radio. Then, I had to go to bed. He turned up the volume just slightly so I could hear the last period from bed.

The last minute of a game, with Montreal down by a goal, was all the drama I could hope to experience. Father would shift into a kind of terror. "Now they've pulled their goalie, Plante is out, those Frenchmen, those Frenchmen will score for sure. They stick together, they get all heated up, and when they need to get a goal, they always get it."

Father was a Toronto Maple Leafs fan. I liked the Detroit Red Wings.

I played hockey until I was twelve or thirteen. Father came to some of my games, not all of them. He rationed the number of games he watched because he loved hockey so much. He thought he should control what could easily become an addiction. He didn't shout like a lot of fathers do now.

He was a stark figure standing on a snowbank behind the boards of the outdoor rink. If I scored, and glanced at him, he would be looking somewhere else. I knew he was proud inside. I learned not to turn to him.

6. CHOIRS CAN BE MAGNIFICENT. You can lose yourself in a choir; both as a member of it, and as one of the audience. Although solos can go dismally wrong, they touch me in a way choirs can't. Solos are not social. They are high risk. They don't fool you. A choir can fool you.

7. I WAS ABOUT SEVENTEEN. Ralph and I were talking theology. I must have been in a contrary mood. We were walking down Reimer Avenue; I said that maybe hell existed after all. Ralph got

angry at this. He wasn't angry about my believing in hell; he knew I didn't really believe that. It was my "againstness," how I had to be "other."

There is a Low German word for this. It says something about me.

Later, it may have been the same day, I grabbed Ralph's Yankee hat and threw it into a tree. He grabbed mine and threw it too. We laughed.

8. RALPH AND I USED TO VISIT, occasionally, with a member of our home church. He must have been maybe eight years older than us, probably twenty-six or so. We could talk about anything with him. He had a marvellous library.

I borrowed *The Dynamics of Faith* by Paul Tillich. I had never read anything like that before. A landmark for me. I first read Kierkegaard here, as well. I didn't enjoy him as much. At the time I didn't feel connected with his mind.

Thinking about it now, I know I had a similar reaction to writers like Sartre and, at least partially, to Kafka. I wondered what it was that held them back. As if each of them came to a barrier on the street and spent the rest of their lives fighting there.

I did enjoy some of Kafka's short stories. "The Country Physician" was crazy, and it struck home. I loved the horses looking in at the window.

Although I first read Graham Greene's *Brighton Rock* in this library, I read primarily nonfiction. Buber, a little Bonhoeffer, various German philosophers, writings by, or about, people like Bakunin and so on.

At the time many of these books were fresh, friendly breezes to me. There were so many possibilities. One could do wonderful things with the mind. When hitched to feelings and desire in a young man, it seemed ideas could go anywhere. I was eclectic and never learned to separate out the systems these writers might have. I took what I wanted, an idea, a series of ideas, an image, a word even, and I fused it all together. It made sense to me.

I guess some of these writers, especially philosophers, eventually made me shake my head. I wondered how they could claim to be objective, how they could say their lives were somehow separate from the linguistic products of their minds. Poets, usually, didn't bother with that kind of dysfunction.

Gerard Manley Hopkins's "Carrion Comfort" left me stunned.

Our friend was a compassionate man with a fine intellect. I learned from the books in his library but, more importantly, I learned from him. I think I am only beginning to apply some of his lessons; how to let the ego have its place, but its place only; how to tolerate the worst, as well as the best, in people; maybe, how to slough off words like worst and best.

He kept his fairly serious differences with the church private. When we asked why, he said he believed in the brotherhood. He was not better than the next man, he said. He didn't have a corner on truth, and there was much to be gained in submitting oneself to a union of fellow believers.

I guess I never fully understood this. Still, I had great respect for him.

9. I LOVE THOSE VOICES THAT TALK of the real world, not the one we have manufactured out of ideas, authority, and arrogance. I don't love the voices that seek power. I love those voices that will not be committed to any cause but continue to speak what no one speaks and hold sacred the world that falls in the cracks. I love fearless voices.

10. I HAVE GONE THROUGH A RANGE OF EMOTIONS about the heritage I was born into, and I have been confused by this heritage. What is it? What was it?

Religiously, I'm not Mennonite. Does this simply mean I'm not a Mennonite? After all, a majority of Mennonites in the world come from other racial groupings than the one I'm from. Yet, I grew up with that name, with a religious, cultural, and linguistic heritage hooked to that name. Some days I feel Mennonite, other days not. It doesn't really matter. It's all in the connotations.

I was born into this. I could have been born elsewhere to different people. That's how it goes. I could have been born in Spain.

Interim: Essays & Mediations

Haircut

DID HE MARK IT ON A CALENDAR? The way, like clockwork, father announced it was time for a haircut. Why today? What was suddenly different? Had there been a revelation?

A board across the armrests of my sister's high-chair and me hoisted up. A dish towel draped around my neck and fastened at the back with a safety pin.

I hated haircuts.

A woman's hair was her glory. Yet she had to cover up in church. Men cropped their hair. They bared their heads.

At some moment, a moment only father seemed to know, my hair was abruptly too long. A moment, apparently, when manliness was lost. But what about all the men in the Bible? They had long hair. Samson's strength lay in his.

Mine was shorn to brushcut length. Later, I understood there was a connection between a shaven head and the loss of individuality. If you joined the army, they cut your hair. Or, if you went to prison.

Or, some holy men. All nuns, we were told, were shaved beneath their coifs. Submission implied. To God, to the church. If a woman's hair was her glory, I could only assume nuns had their heads shaved to eliminate all vestiges of personal glory and pride. To dedicate themselves utterly to God and church.

The loss of self, and a dedication to something higher.

Van Gogh in his last self-portraits. Looking like a lice-infested convict. The elimination of self?

Dedication to his art? A prisoner of his art. It could be called dedication, but which came first?

Dedication, or imprisonment? Did he loathe himself?
In the '60s we let our hair grow. We gloried in it. The freedom of
hair swaying as you moved. Blessed in the natural world.
A little god, and why not, walking down Main Street with leath-
er boots and long hair. Free at last. From restraints and propriety.
Having lived in the '50s, in a small town.
Stood against the armies of the world. We thought. Stood
against bureaucrats, conformists, bean-counters, ministers, what-
ever. We thought.
And yet, van Gogh. That suffering face. A man with too much love
for his own good. A man without defences. A musical instrument con-
stantly played upon. By fellow humans, family, the streets of European
cities, by the vineyards and radiating sun of southern France.
A convict like that. Not a saint. But a man with the compassion
and heart of an artist.

The cloth around my throat was always too tight. I'd beg father
to loosen it. He'd comb my hair. His touch, at first, smooth and
gentle. My hair flying with static.

No matter how careful he was, the clippers tugged at my hair. A
young boy crying out, involuntarily moving his head. The scissors.
More clippers. More tugged hair. A restless boy. Hair falling into
my eyes, on my nose, and in. Imprisoned hands unable to scratch.
Going crazy.

With each new movement, father straightened me a little less
carefully. I could feel a violence running through his hands. An
increasing irritation. Trying to give me a decent cut, his idea of a
decent cut. Civilizing me. The boy squirming and complaining. And
hating every second of it.

Until, finally, father blurted out in anger a final command to be
still. His fingers digging into my shoulders. Then, my tears.

Cursing him beneath my breath, cursing the haircut. The shear-
ing of sheep. Remembering how he said it hurt him too when his
father cut his hair. His father a farmer with a rough hand.

Thinking of the marvel, the wonder of each of us. Destined for
various scrap heaps.

Grandfather an old man on a boney field. Grandmother in a
black and red Russian shawl. Father in the single-minded hurry of
middle life. My cousin carving a slingshot in the shade of a willow.

Interim: Essays & Mediations

Thinking of Jesus or Mohammed or Siddhartha. Earning their way. With one eye on heaven. In our day rising out of the grey middle classes, rock or movie stars. Some genius, a lot of illusion. Flash.

Mother Theresa. From Albania. Refusing to be a star, and so becoming one. Rising beyond the everyday magazine faces. Another world altogether.

Dickinson at the window. Tsvetaeva in the doorway. O'Neill bathing his wounds in the sea. Gould's fingers. Schumann on the bridge.

Wondering why we don't remember, each day, the fire in each of us. The suffering. The delight. The songs.

It doesn't prevent us ending up on one scrap heap or another. But, it can shine a light where light is needed, give shade where light need not be.

". . . the light is too dark. . . ."

Says my son, aged six, at twilight.

This must be some version of Goethe. Or Pasternak who wanted the window open as he died.

After father had blown stray hairs from my neck with the warmth of his breath; after he carefully removed the cloth and shook it outside; after an impatient supper, I dressed in my costume, and grandmother painted my face. Then, an old flour sack in hand, I joined my friends to venture into the dark of Hallowe'en.

The cool evening. Leaves underfoot. Feet crunching across brown lawns, distant voices calling at doors and windows. The orange flicker of candles. Opening my bag for apples or caramels. Comparing loot. Shortcuts through shrubs. Moving into light, up porch steps, and calling in unison.

"Hallowe'en apples."

Avoiding the teacher's house because he made us sing. Avoiding a dark house with sagging shutters where an old brother and sister lived. Recluses. With warts. Mother said they were alcoholics.

My charcoal face, with dark, thick eyebrows, and wild hair. An old familiarity.

On the porch of another house. A Godly man. Us calling out like a children's choir, in unison. "Hallowe'en apples."

Him heaving to the door. A shape in the hall behind the door's frosted glass. The door swinging open, and him standing there, hunched.

Staring at this little gypsy band. Angry. His eyes finding me at the front of the group.

"Is that the face God gave you?"

Saying, "what do you mean?" before I realized he meant the face my grandmother had painted on me.

"No, grandmother made my face."

"She did, did she? Is she God? And why did she make a devil out of you? Can you tell me that?"

"Well. . . ."

"Because that's what you are. A devil. That's not the face God gave you. You've changed what you were given. Come, I'll wipe it off. Quickly. Before the devil takes you over."

I backed off, frightened. Of his intensity. His unearthly eyes. Wondering if he was right. Was it possible? Could I become a devil because my face was painted?

Did he see a true me? What was stirring inside? An uncoiling, an appetite. My eyes not on heaven at all, but on earth. Just beginning to realize how much I loved the world. Realizing I couldn't see God, only things from God.

We stood there, dumbly. He noticed our open bags.

"Boys, do you really think I could give you anything? Tonight of all nights, when Satan's in the air, and you're in his power. It's the Devil's day. Not God's. A heathenish day. Don't you know it's Satan's way of winning your souls? Come in, let me wipe off your faces."

African masks. Voodoo and dance. Feathers, bones, blood. Earthly cries. Transformations.

In full retreat. Halfway down his driveway. Away from the light falling from his doorway. And, finally, turning and fleeing across the street.

Still hearing his last words, his aching voice reaching for song. "'Tis so sweet to trust in Jesus."

And we were gods, yes, little devils, leaping through the night. Clear-eyed and unfathomable. Not ourselves. All ancient memory, and before.

Feathers, bones, blood. Charcoal faces. And the fire.

Standing, later, in my backyard at the edge of the light the kitchen window threw. Wondering. And leaving, I think; leaving home. The board leaning against the house, a few hairs clinging to it.

Without a Bow Tie

I HAVE NO FORMAL POETICS. I have spoken about poetics, written about it, and I have contradicted myself. What seems clear one day is not on another. Then, something that was unclear, or even invisible, suddenly emerges. My capacity to organize all this into some kind of coherent poetics is practically nil. I don't think its organization is of any benefit to anyone, particularly to me.

I write poems, but I'm not sure I'm a poet, or whether what I write is poetry. Who defines it? What does it mean? I am astonished by many poets, knowing I cannot write as they do. But, then, I wonder why I would even think for a moment that I should. Undoubtedly, I use certain techniques, some with long tradition, some more recent. I know I'm not very consistent.

Just speaking. Where I'm from, as far as I'm aware, and where I'm going, as far as I'm aware. Trying to be awake to what's inside, and to what's around me. I've learned from many. I don't break any new ground. It's all been said and done.

What I'm interested in is the immediacy of poems. Something approaching improvisation, and yet shaped for page and voice. No explanations needed. A voice spoken and heard.

I play music while I write. When the CD runs out, and I don't remember having heard most of it, it's probably been a pretty good writing session. And when I do hear the music, let's say when I pause, it's important what I'm hearing. So, I program my CD player with music that I think best interacts with what I am writing. The musical selections are all over the map, from sacred music like Mozart's *Ave verum corpus* and Russian Orthodox choirs to fado to Bill Evans to The Band.

I use pale blue paper to print the poems. I'm not sure why. I think it's pleasing to my eye. The words are less stark there, less formal; they're stark enough as it is. Typically I tend to write late and into the early hours of morning. The robot, within, is asleep then. Things flow. Thinking, words, the senses alive. With the music playing quietly, I step onto my balcony, and it feels like I'm the only person alive on earth. Until a siren wails down Commercial Drive, or someone stumbles down the sidewalk. Even, then, I'm alone in some serene way.

Someone said that you had to practically wear a bow tie to listen to classical music these days. A suggestion of the end of the improvisational, associational, spontaneity of the early stages of art forms. I don't want to ever wear a bow tie when I write or read my work. I've got this one time around, and I intend to use the language I have learned, to speak, on the page and in performance, what I am and know, to remember. Leaving some evidence behind.

There Was Always Music

FROM THE BEGINNING THERE WAS MUSIC. Can't remember a time it wasn't there in one form or another. Probably the greatest constant in my life. Mother was always singing. Hymns sometimes but often English folk songs, Scottish and Irish ballads. She had a fine soprano voice, often sang in church. Once, when she was about twenty-one years old, and me a one-year-old child in my father's lap, she recorded "O Holy City" in some walk-in recording joint on Portage Avenue in Winnipeg. Cost her a dollar or so. I know this happened. I own the recording, the date on it. She also played the piano a lot. Often, at the end of the day, with me lying in bed. Playing me to sleep.

Father whistled and hummed while he worked, or maybe just standing in the basement looking at the beams and joists. He was a carpenter with a builder's eye. I couldn't always identify his songs. Were they old Wilf Carter tunes? I'd heard he once loved Wilf Carter, used to play the guitar and sing his songs. I'd heard he and his brothers yodelled. I never heard them, though. He never talked about it, had left that music behind long before I was born.

The two of them sang together. In the house. Mother might be washing dishes, father drying. One would start a hymn, and the other would join in. Nothing special. Happened all the time. Sometimes his arm around her waist.

They sang in quartets as well. Usually with two relatives. They'd rehearse at our house. Mother playing the piano, singing soprano. Father chewing black liquorice drops for his throat. I remember that medicinal smell. And all of them singing. They'd sing in church, or at the old folks home on Sunday morning, or sometimes at the bedside of an unusual woman, not really old, who had taken to bed at quite a young age and never left. No one knew what her problem was. At least I asked once, and that's what I was told.

Always music, instrumental and vocal. Soprano, piano and baritone. I remember all this like skin knows air. When I stop to think what was the first classical music I ever heard, I think immediately of a bulky package that came through the mail. Mother had ordered it from some record company, through *Reader's Digest*. I remember her opening it. I remember a halo of hair around a scowling face. All the symphonies of Beethoven.

Those were the only classical recordings we had in our house. In fact, we had almost no recordings at all. I don't remember any, until I grew old enough to sneak rock 'n' roll into my room and play it on a seventeen-dollar, one-speed record player under the blankets. Oh, and I do remember a Blackwood Brothers Quartet Gospel album I brought home, hoping that these Gospel singers, a group Elvis Presley had hoped to join, would convince my parents that rock 'n' roll wasn't all that bad. It didn't work.

Usually the music was live, in the house. What do I remember about Beethoven? It could have been the Ninth with those magnificent voices, or it might have been some marvellous moments at the heart of the Eroica. I remember both well, scratches and all. I remember the Seventh, too, the Pastoral.

I never was a big fan of symphonies, though. There is something too grand about them, too immense for my ears. I preferred my mother on the piano. I like a smaller scale, something more intimate. I try to remember my first classical music. I thought it was one of those symphonies. Which came first? Probably the Ninth. But that's a guess.

Meanwhile, I heard rock and loved it. That energy and release. I still like it, though I tend to return to the musicians of my late teens and early twenties. A little later I picked up on jazz. I began with Theolonius Monk, which probably wasn't the most auspicious start. It sounded like he played a note a minute. That was a shock, with me coming from the head-first propulsion of rock. I tried again later. I appreciate Monk now, but I love Bill Evans's trios best of all. Scott LaFaro, Paul Motian and Bill Evans. In fact, I learned a lot about the long line by listening to Bill Evans. I returned to classical music every few years. I began to build a CD collection. I liked quartets, trios, and solo work. I especially loved the voice; Russian Orthodox singing, Schubert *lieder*, Rachmaninoff's "Three Songs," that kind of music.

In the early 1990s I picked up a Robert Schumann CD. Claudio Arrau on piano. The cover said *Carnaval, Kinderszenen* and *Waldszenen*. As far as I remember, now, I had heard some of *Waldszenen* on the radio. The CBC no doubt. It was a piece of Germanic forest Romanticism. Not utterly arresting, but interesting enough for me to want to investigate it.

Typically, I played nothing but the nine pieces of *Waldszenen* for a few weeks, programming my CD player. One evening, as I was working at the typer, I let the whole CD play. Innumerable short pieces of solo piano.

I had to stop at the second note of a new piece. From *Kinderszenen* (Scenes from Childhood). I was astonished. I knew the song instantly. At the second note. That pause after the first. Hanging there. Then that movement up to the second note. I knew it. I was shot back probably forty years in time. Not to any specific place at first. To my childhood. And, as I listened, I knew this was the first piece of classical music I'd ever heard. I looked for its name in the CD booklet. *Träumerei*. Reverie, In Dreams. That was the piece. Remembering.

Me lying in bed, just short of sleep, and mother in the living room, playing piano. Not another sound in the house. The slow notes drifting down the hall through the crack always left open at the door so I could see light. And into my ears.

Such a delicate piece. Romantic, unquestionably. Insubstantial as dreams, insubstantial as childhood remembered. Long ago music reaching back and forth in time. A short lyric, a moment before sleep. That time when you open up, your brain exhausted and not trying to think. Things can happen.

Mother would have been about twenty-six or twenty-seven then. Me, six or seven. Perhaps we were younger.

My first classical music remembered, caught in some fold of my brain. Part of my body. Like I said, from the beginning, there was always music.

Jugular Music

I SPEAK FOR MYSELF. There is no theoretical package here, no system, not necessarily a consistency, but probably eccentricity. I have a strong aversion, physically, spiritually, and mentally, for ideology. These are a handful of thoughts and feelings about poetry, its place, its process. Poetry is dear to me. I grew up with it, in one form or another. Ballads, poems, the Bible, Schubert, hymns. It's a way of thinking, a way of being. It's life-blood. Jugular music.

A few years ago I noticed that the stack of new books I had bought and not yet read was piling up rapidly. After about a year there must have been forty to fifty books. Thinking about it, I realized my relationship to books was changing.

Remember how you latched onto a particular writer? Anaïs Nin, perhaps, or Joyce, or Hemingway. For me, now, there are few "must-reads." I rarely key on authors and read all their books voraciously. I remember when books seemed to change my life. I still read a lot, but nothing clicks the way it used to. Very little seems fresh or original.

I thought perhaps I was becoming illiterate. Is that what happens with aging? Does one reach a reading peak and then reverse and move steadily back to illiteracy, or rather pre-literacy? Of course, this isn't literally what happens.

I talked to my friend Per who was experiencing the same thing. I read an essay on the phenomenon in a magazine. There didn't seem to be an answer to the mystery. Perhaps there's something in the publishing industry, the hype, the book of the year tripe, the various jousts for literary supremacy, that's draining the life out of books, making them exclusively commercial, part of an entertainment industry; reduced to a product like everything else.

I remember when a new book had a smell to it, a marvellous smell from the printers. First thing I did when one of my books came out was smell it. Then I'd feel the texture of the cover and riff through the pages examining the font. It was a sensual experience. It's less so now.

Perhaps, one simply reads one's fill and becomes jaded. Perhaps writing has deteriorated, and there's not much worth reading. We are becoming an industry, not a calling. Being a writer may be almost as much about publicity, interviews, pronouncements on television and radio, as it is about the process of creating with words.

Whatever the answers, it has made me think about books, about the writing and reading of them. For me, what works, what doesn't, and why.

Certainly, in poetry, there has not been very much that has seized me in some time. Too much of it is unmusical, unfelt, at best a cleverness, a working out of some puzzle. Much of it doesn't matter to me. And, if it doesn't matter, why read it?

Milosz, in his eighties and heading toward his nineties, got better and better, and less and less intellectual. An old man returning to simplicity, the simplicity of someone who has lived a full life and returns to the intelligence of the child. There are other poets who still appeal to me, here and away, but the list is short. Most of them are older than me.

So, how to begin. With the feel. The interrelatedness of everything. I take my cues from music. Rhythm and image. I want the feel. Poetry begins there, I think, in human feeling. That's where the fire is lit.

It's lit in the child, that wide-eyed wonder; then it's doused, as we're formed into citizens; and, often, it glows again in old age. Direct experiences. No self-censorship, fearless.

New music happens when there's a need, not when someone decides it's time. This century jazz had to happen, given the complexity of cultural realities in the United States. Untutored formally, it took elements from the past, including ragtime, gospel and blues, and went in a new direction, growing into its own depth, through swing and improvisation into bebop and beyond. It became something different when critics wrote about it, explained it.

Patrick Friesen   33

Rock, too, had to happen. Again, untutored, felt out of a web of religion and culture, tearing free to a degree, flaming brightly. Then possessed by the producers, the money people. They try to perpetuate it, start new trends, create new stars. Sometimes, it makes them a lot of money, but there's no depth, no vital emerging out of tradition, no staying power.

People still listen to Louis Armstrong and Charlie Parker, Presley, the Beatles. The moment of ecstasy they each were, the feel. Until the next moment.

I'm listening to a CD of Elvis Presley's *Sun Sessions*. These are the very first records he made, before he achieved fame and a slow disintegration into cult religious status. By today's standards these records are almost primitively recorded. There is, however, something absolutely fresh, exciting, energetic, emotional, humorous and direct about these early records. "That's Alright Mama" sounds guileless. Simple human expression on a popular level.

Charlie Parker, essentially self-taught, finding out at his first jam in Kansas City that there was more than one key to play in. Going home to learn all the keys. If he'd listened, he would have found he only needed three or four keys. He taught himself all twelve. Changing jazz with his improvising, his search for the "feel" in each song he played.

Or, listen to Sandy Denny; Richard Manuel singing almost anything. Listen to an old scratchy record of the Spanish singer of Cante Jondo, La Niña De Los Peines, singing "Agonia," or Lucília do Carmo, the Portuguese *fadista*, singing "Maria Madalena." Listen to Miles Davis replacing La Niña's voice with his trumpet on "Saeta" on the *Sketches of Spain* album. Listen to yodelling or falsetto. Listen to whistling. Who whistles now? Listen to Sonny Rollins playing his saxophone's mouthpiece only on "East Broadway Rundown," terrifyingly human. Uilleann pipes with a tin whistle, "Amazing Grace" by almost anyone, or Keith Jarrett humming imperfection into his music.

Unselfconscious and felt.

Like childhood. Like the best of our art, our poetry. Something direct, unmediated, body to body, tongue to ear, human breath. Something so honest that even if you don't understand all of it, you trust it, you listen because you know you can understand it. Besides, you are understanding at a non-analytical, non-verbal level. Absorbing it, body and mind. In contrast, a possibly apocryphal story: a musician told me recently that Schoenberg reached a point where he said he could no longer explain his music, so he quit playing and composing. Theory, the intellect, seen as the only legitimate source of art. The labyrinth of intellect. Is this what Milton called hell? The intellect, like the actor staring into a mirror, enamoured of itself, becoming convinced it's the only reality. John Gardner wrote, "intellect is the chief distracter of the mind."

Theory has its place. In the cart behind the horse. Or, as Tom Stoppard observed: "It is a mistake to assume that my plays are the end product of ideas. The ideas are the end product of the plays."

All writers work with ideas, experiment with form, but they don't necessarily build intellectual cathedrals. Critics and theorists look for patterns and consistencies in literature. They look for what holds together, what doesn't, from that particular point of view. This can be interesting, even valuable, for readers and writers. As long as it keeps its place as a reflective analysis exploring, in its limited fashion, what has already been written. Even then, in the hands of those with some authority within the writing community, it can wreak havoc with those poets not belonging to the right church.

Some people need ideology, an intellectual construct that explains things to them, not only things they don't understand otherwise, but things they don't seem to want to understand on any level but the ideological. The perfect map that explains everything. And they need to control, dominate the field. There's an astonishing narrowness of thought here they don't recognize. A narrowness of interpretation and imagination.

Reminding me of the minor theological differences among some of the churches in my home town. One church argued that to be properly baptized you had to be dunked in a tank or some shallow river. Another church countered with the sufficiency of sprinkling on the crown of the head. In fact, the Essenes, who apparently first baptized believers, would hold a person's head underwater to the point of losing consciousness and possibly dying. The full experience of death by water and the possible visions of an oxygen-starved brain.

Dunking or sprinkling. The pale theories go on. The building of cathedrals. And, then, the question of who gets in, who doesn't.

Who decides? Some academics, said Doris Lessing in a radio interview, think they hold the keys to literature. No one cometh to the literature but by them. As one such academic said to me after I mentioned how much I, and the rest of the audience, had enjoyed a recent Leonard Cohen concert, "The trouble with Cohen is that he gives all those fans the impression they know something about poetry." The great unwashed.

One may or may not like Cohen, may or may not know much about poetics, no problem there; it's the arrogance and elitism of this "holder of the keys" attitude that is a real threat to poetry. The distancing of poetry from people. The reduction of poetry to a theoretical game that may keep them employed. And the failure to know that poetry is rooted in song. When theory imposes itself on literature, when writers begin to write according to the ideology they've bought into, a kind of death has begun. This is not to deny change, that happens in spite of us, but it is to deny the domination of arbitrary theories held by a relatively small number of people who do indeed hold some keys, not to literature, but to positions of authority and influence.

Those without an over-arching theory, those who might identify with the poet accused, a few years ago, by a Canadian literary theorist, of being "resistant to theory," could, in the past, simply not pay attention and get on with their writing. As there's less money for publishers, journals, and literary grants, they do so at their peril now.

It seems to me, there's a fear among those who aren't part of a network of literary theoreticians, to voice their disagreements, to point out the little tyrannies that exist. Is it the fear of ridicule, of being shut out of whatever chances they have for a grant, a publication, a trip to Europe? The fear they won't be part of the necessary network? I don't know. It may simply be the fear so many of us have in the contemporary world, the fear of being wrong, the fear of risk, the fear of being labelled something disagreeable, the fear of offending one interest group or another. Correctness is rife in our society, and nowhere more so than in many areas of academia.

Biting one's tongue. Having been taught that intellectuals are more intelligent than the rest of us. How could one have anything to say? One should be valuing one's personal experience, which includes studying and learning, knowing its immediacy to be far finer material, and truer, for poetry than the narrowing of risk and vision in ideology. Biting one's tongue.

Ideology dies. Poetry, so far, hasn't. In countries dominated by tyrannies, time and again, people survived physically because they survived spiritually. Often this was because of poetry, that balance of intellect and feeling. That music.

Marina Tsvetaeva and Anna Akhmatova in the Soviet Union. Highly intelligent poets writing out of a harmony of mind and heart, body and soul. Yes, engaging in literary arguments, but always the whole human writing to the whole human listening. An immediacy. A need to write, and a need to hear. Human stories, human emotions and thoughts. Accessible words.

Akhmatova was part of a group of poets called Acmeists. They were a group of like-minded poets who discussed, and argued over, poetic form and content. Mechanics talking about engines (a good mechanic loves his work, is fascinated by its process, but his aim is to make a car run). A necessary activity for her to stay on top of her work. But she didn't write for them; she didn't write for the approval of an incestuous group of other poets and critics; she wrote for the people of Russia. And, complex as her work might get, it always remained accessible to everyone in her culture. Although the ruling bureaucrats viciously attacked her for the emotional content of her poems, her audience kept reading her. She spoke to that place of spirit and feeling that was being atrophied by the state. Her work remains, the state lies in ruins, still causing an afterword of damage.

Poets and words. Trying to use words to explore and communicate the ancient, never-ending human concerns, joys and humours, directly and freshly. Intelligence, not intellect. As in the pre-revolutionary Russian intelligentsia, where intellectualism was not necessary to belong; an unschooled poet, like Esenin, whose verses moved common people, could be included. We, too, in different circumstances, can atrophy.

I'll listen to Nina Simone singing "Ne Me Quitte Pas" or "The Last Rose of Summer." I'll take the intelligence inherent in "Peace Piece" by Bill Evans. And Gwendolyn MacEwen reciting from the *T. E. Lawrence Poems* at Mary Scorer Bookstore in Winnipeg in 1983.

Accessible poetry. Imagery and music, comparisons, relationships. Thought and feeling. A poem does not have to be explained. It speaks for itself. It says exactly what it means. It isn't philosophy, theology, economics, literary theory, or politics in fancy clothes. All these things can exist within poems, but they don't explain the process.

The poem has to have an emotional component, a rhythmic component. It must appeal to more than the intellect, be more than a page exercise. It doesn't worry about contradictions, has no need to become a theory. Poetry gestates. It uses language, with all its resonance, to attempt to understand the whole human in the natural world, in the world humanly created. In the intersections between the two. It explores, reveals, weeps, praises.

Poetry, for me, has a quality of what D. H. Lawrence called "in-betweeness." It lives between the lines and lies. It straddles intellect and emotion. It is interested in what falls in the cracks, not necessarily in what receives attention. It keeps alive what is being forgotten, what is broken.

A stone, a reed. A yellow-headed blackbird. These are things I remember, things I know, in a way. For me, poetry is the process of knowing, not so much the end knowledge.

William Irwin Thompson, in *The Imagination of an Insurrection*, said, "By refusing to commit himself to political action the artist is insisting on discovering what he senses has been ignored in the politician's demand for an immediate commitment. . . ." I understand politics in a broad sense here.

Authority always behaves the same way. It needs to close, even as it says it's doing the opposite. It needs to contain and shape everything for its own end; it is not comfortable with the undefined, with the loose moment, the full intake of breath.

I'm tired of seeing poems with endless brackets and parentheses breaking compound words into their component parts. I know how words are constructed. I'm bored by writers reminding me that they're writing the book, or poem, I'm reading. I'm tired not only of literary theory being imposed on poetry but, also, the theories of various social and political causes.

Ethnicity, gender, deconstruction, post-structuralism, post-colonialism, and others. If any of these things are carried within the larger poem, fine; there are necessary truths anywhere, even if they are partial. To hell with them, though, when they issue marching orders to the poet or the reader. Ideology kills. Resistant to theory? Damn right.

Poetry undermines and sabotages authority simply by existing. It resists categorization and manipulation. A moment of process, utilizing what is already known, and giving voice to what is voiceless.

I love the complex simplicity of a Japanese haiku, as far as I can understand it in English. Or the diary entry of an unimportant person. Chekhov's father wrote: "A peony blossomed in the garden. Maria Petrovna came. The peony faded. Maria Petrovna left."

Simplicity and freshness. The words of an amateur. I love to hear the guitarist's fingers on the fret board. I love to hear the poet's breath. I love to hear them work. Watching the dance from backstage. Direct, not self-censoring. Perhaps we need the amateur again. The amateur poet. Something felt and intelligent and expressed in a form true to that feel. A balance. And a trust in our personal experience.

Saul Bellow said in an interview: "there have been tremendous mistakes in thought, but the worst of all was the casting out of all connection with one's own nature and one's own knowledge. Private knowledge has in it a rare kind of truth. . . ."

Enough quotes. Even in quoting these various artists I'm falling back on what we're taught to do, appeal to authority. Why not simply speak out of personal experience? If what is spoken is stupid, it will be so judged. Authority doesn't make anything more true. There is, I guess, a reassurance in quoting other artists, a feeling of not being alone. And, often, there is the pleasure of hearing one's incomplete thoughts expressed beautifully by others. Like Bill Evans spontaneously quoting someone else's composition within one of his. The fun of it, the endless interrelatedness of things.

I don't know. But I do. I know what works for me. You know what works for you. Not cleverness, but the truth you know when you hear it, read it.

The truth of your wide-awake, unafraid intelligence. The poetry that speaks fully to you. Where you don't have to calculate whether your network, your school, approves or not.

I'm not saying all writing, all poets, are equally good. Not at all; they're not. The writing of poetry may be a democratic activity; the creation of an excellent poem is not. I believe poetry is a calling, as are other ways of seeing and understanding the world. A calling in how one individual knows to see the world, hear it fully, and try to pass on a little of what is possible.

Not a calling announced with trumpets, but a finding out. And if you become a good poet, it doesn't place you on a pedestal. You have your work, that's all. You are not a brain surgeon with a steady hand, nor are you a carpenter with a carpenter's eye. You are not a cultural worker. You are a poet, though you may often doubt it.

You have to remain accessible. Not simplistic, not stupid, not some versifier. Accessible. Speaking well, poetically. Not writing in the stratosphere, but not writing down to people either. Coming through and being heard.

Writing as prayer, an interior conversation with god knows whom or what. With the numerous selves I am? The Lord? Who's that? What I know is that when I was a young, first-time father, and my six-month old daughter Marijke in a high fever, I feared. I held her to my bare chest; I was cooler by far than she was, and she found it comforting. When she finally fell asleep, I went to my room to write a poem. It was a prayer for my child. It wasn't written to be published; in fact, I destroyed it once she was well. It was a prayer to a greater power I knew firsthand as I wrote. Letting go, giving it over to whatever it was I talked with when I wrote. In the process, as always, I found a stillness.

I've always had these interior conversations, since I was a child. Later, they became poems. I don't know who I speak with, but it's intimate; there is knowing back and forth. This conversation is only possible if I let go into the process and, I believe, if I don't name the other. Once I explain and name, it's gone. That's how it works, always has, for me. As a poet, I let go to the world, its objects, and am possessed by them. Then I can write. As an Anabaptist theologian said long ago, "comprehending the invisible through the visible." In the end, it seems, we all have to let go of the world that has been an utter presence all our lives. That is an awesome loss. Or, maybe not. I'll find out.

There is mystery in the world, in spirit, in poetry. There are, among the hours of tough work, moments we call inspiration. Why deny this? Why fear it? Poetry is nothing but learning the right tricks in schools, in workshops? Please. Can anyone become an excellent athlete, a fine surgeon, as long as he or she gets the right training?

Throughout history there has been an acceptance of inspiration, the taking in of breath. Receiving the ghost. Inhalation. The word covers a lot of human experience.

Like the Essenes' baptisms, poetry, whether humorous or serious, is life and death stuff. It shifts perceptions, changes lives. Jugular music.

Poetry is powerless. Like the child, or old age. Answering to no authority.

Poetry, Again

THERE IS NO ONE WAY OF KNOWING POETRY, whether by that is meant definition or intimacy. For me it has been there as long as I remember. Sometimes it took the form of songs, and the voice of the singer. It also took the form of the odd sermon, and I mean that literally. Ultimately it was simply the fact of my love of the sound, the physical implications, of words. A back and forth between earth's things and words.

When the language was rooted in the physical, in my experience of being alive, body and soul, then I discovered that poetry was subversive in the most fundamental way. It subverted me. Like a posed photograph which presents an approximation of the subject. Be there, hiding nothing, while the shutter opens for a second, and you will remain forever hidden; the photo a physical representation to provoke memory and strangeness. The photographer can always attempt to subvert the pose, or possibly find something "else" within the pose. The various selves, even the one caught, unaware, on the move.

Poetry is a fine sanity. Anything can happen there; it is not risk-free territory. Poetry comes from a wild place and is shifted into form of one kind or another. That shifting is the work of the poet, and it entails dives into some dark pools or, changing metaphors, a singeing of the hair and hands; it involves an undercutting of self and its intentions. I write out of my many limitations, personal and poetic. It's here, at my limit, that things become possible, that I can actually arrive at something authentic. You just have to leave the learning behind sometimes and get stupid. For me, poetry is not right-angled.

"How Like an Angel Came I Down!"

I LOVE THE ENDING. I wish I'd written it. It seems obvious enough now, like it's been done somewhere before. Maybe it has. The nerve of it. Thinking of the ceiling in a stage play. Balconies, ladders, stairs, yes. But a ceiling? Another wall. A wall to heaven. Heaven, or outer space, taken so naturalistically.

I love this ending. Seeing it, hearing it, the sheer physicality of it in the Walter Kerr Theatre. A moment with incredible resonances for the senses and the imagination. A moment to take off on.

"How like an angel came I down!" *

An ending that speaks at once of release, salvation, death, prophecy, and the endless opening up of human possibility, transcendence. An ending that speaks of birth.

Angels in America, a visitation from another sphere, another kind of power than Americans are accustomed to. Avenging angel, or stern, an embracing angel. It's not one angel in the title, it's angels. Battalions of them, like UFOs. Blue Angels, maybe, like some acrobatic air force squadron of jet fighters. Guardian angels, holding hands, the blue ring of the ozone layer.

More likely, angels inherent, a birthing, the becoming of angels.

"How like an angel came I down!"

The play is about limits. The limits of humanity, its ultimate powerlessness in the face of nature. Disease and death as nature's great levellers.

Roy Cohn, with all his politics and telephones, with venereal warts up his ass. He squirms over semantics, sociological hierarchies, and

---

* The line is from "Wonder" by Thomas Traherne (1636-74).

power politics, but he can't escape his human vulnerability. Though he hides it under a barrage of obscenity and power brokerage.

A priggish church; the vulgar offices of its power. How it binds the individual in its community and in the rigidity of its doctrine. How it judges and condemns precisely what is most human.

The lonely, violent park bench. The desperate couch.

You can almost hear Joe's skeleton clatter. So little flesh on him, so little give and take. His whole being bent toward the squeaky-clean machine someone else decreed as model. The unbearable pressure of that.

Paralleled by the skinniness of Prior. Physical and spiritual star-vations. Prior and Joe. Harper's dreams of snow. Her despair, her valium, her yearning for another world. She knows everything is collapsing, "systems of defence giving way. . . ." (p. 17)*

The angel plummeting into the dying man's bedroom. Music and celestial light. Smoke and rending. The ceiling breaking open.

Divine intervention or human transcendence. Are they two different concepts? Or, simply, two namings of the same experience? God's hand reaching down; human arms rising. Prayer and answer, supplication and comfort.

"How like an angel came I down!" wrote Thomas Traherne in the seventeenth century.

I that so long
Was nothing from eternity. . . .**

The angel as child within us. The child, as yet uncorrupted by culture, all its agents. The angel as human deity.

Prior has been told by a beautiful voice to look up. A grey feath-er has floated down to him. Is this what he is to look for? His own purity, the wisdom of his own long-forgotten divinity? The innate goodness of human beings?

Does an obscenity like Cohn hold a child inside? Is it possible to be so corrupted, so broken down, the child is destroyed? This is the

---

* Page references are to *Angels in America* by Tony Kushner.
New York: Theatre Communications Group, 1993.
** Thomas Traherne, "The Salutation."

question of salvation and redemption. And is there a way back?

The Christian doctrine of original sin made human. We are born, corrupted, and can be redeemed, not through intrusion from outside somewhere, but through a return to the innocence of infancy. Individual, self-contained redemption; heaven inherent in us.

Prior is each of us. He has been prior and will be again. The wheel turning; the repeating process of birth, earthly fall, death, and birth again.

Nature, and the human construction banging into nature, is the fall. As if we are from two different sources; as if we are not part of nature.

Prior and his disease. Not a disease of culture, though it takes cultural forms. Disease is always natural. Only its forms keep shifting. Disease is opportunistic; it takes what is given, sex, religion, pollution, antibiotics, whatever, and does nature's work.

Whoever, whatever, we want to blame for any given disease is irrelevant. Such a strange human activity, pointing fingers amongst ourselves, to find a scapegoat on whom to hang the blame. What better villain than the victim?

"He's sick; he must have done something to deserve it." The summoners speak.

The voice of ideology. That kind of rigidity, the overlaying of some mental, ideal construct upon the flesh and blood man and woman breathing, eating, defecating, loving and dying.

We die. That's it. Nature.

We all die. Do we deserve it? Does that make any sense? A kind of value system attached to disease and death; degrees of guilt, fine shadings of judgement. Elaborate grids of faith and belief to proclaim eternal life.

We can live and die as angels. Or, not. Is that what we mean by freedom?

Human culture recognizing its foundation, the wheel of nature, and choosing to build goodness, compassion, and dignity upon that ground. Not the freedom away from something, but a freedom toward; the freedom to be rooted, as a tree, or as a bird is held by sky.

There is something comic here, as well. The angel does not pass lightly through the roof; nothing ghostly, no transformation, no osmosis. The angel is heavily physical, crashing through plaster and lathe-work. A clumsiness, slapstick even. Prior, hearing the music, seeing the light show, gives the event a humorous cultural framework.

"God almighty. . . . *Very* Stephen Spielberg" (p. 118).

The effervescence of American culture meeting eternal verities.

That distance in Prior, the contemporary American man. That capacity, that need, to diminish what is serious, even final. A postmodern sabotage; a fear; the decision to not face the hollow within, the angel banished, but to project this emptiness onto the world, and announce the world desolate and void of meaning.

This is not comedy as relief, but comedy as despair. It's a tightening of the screws; a rejection of nature, and a full embrace of culture.

Greetings, Prophet;
The Great Work begins:
The Messenger has arrived (p. 119).

Whose messenger? Messenger of what news? And, what is the Great Work?

Nature has sent innumerable messages through its workings. Humans have seen nature's work, nature's responses to human greed, human arrogance and ignorance. Nature, without intentions, carries on. We see and learn, or we don't. No matter; nature is relentless.

We only see the message in forms our imagination is taught to read. Divine intervention. The metaphor of divinity; our imaginative construct for what we don't accept in nature, what we attribute to some Higher Being.

Yes, this could be an angel from heaven. Yes, it could be what we want to see. What we fear, and what we hope for. The intervention, the inevitability of nature, turning around human gall. The celestial event that holds the mystery, giving us an out.

As Prior says to Harper, "I usually say, 'Fuck the truth,' but mostly, the truth fucks you" (p. 34). The truths of nature, and the truths of human experience as built up through time.

The angel delivers a message of apocalypse to Prior. In his disease, Prior embodies the prophecy, the Great Work of decimation.

Earlier, Prior has told his departing lover, Louis, a story of an early ancestor.

A ship's captain, this ancestor went down in a winter storm near Nova Scotia. Seventy survivors, mostly women and children, rode in a leaky longboat. Each time the water rose too high in the boat, the crew members would grab the nearest passengers and hurl them out into the cold ocean. Until the ballast was right again. By the time the boat arrived in Halifax, nine of the original seventy people remained.

> PRIOR: I think about that story a lot now. People in a boat, waiting, terrified, while implacable, unsmiling men, irresistibly strong, seize . . . maybe the person next to you, maybe you, and with no warning at all, with time only for a quick intake of air you are pitched into freezing, turbulent water and salt and darkness to drown (p. 42).

The lesson is obvious. The sacrifice of the most vulnerable so the strong will survive. Contemporary society, its dominant members, and those suffering from AIDS. In Prior's case, even his lover deserts him. The ruthless business of survival.

This story is central to the play. This is how the apocalypse happens. This is the thinning out of society, the Darwinian procedure.

The angel crashing through the ceiling. The messenger from afar. An alien, an angel. Doom and the end of things, apocalypse. And the opening up of the sky. The possibility of transcendence.

Prior, at the end of his story, admits that he is drawn to Louis' cosmology, Louis' escape from the hard facts, and yet finds this escape a ducking of responsibility.

"While time is running out I find myself drawn to anything that's suspended, that lacks an ending but it seems to me that it lets you off scot-free" (p. 42).

The angel is suspended above the world of this play until the very end. The sound of distant wings, a beautiful voice speaking to Prior, a grey feather floating down from the ceiling, foreshadow the epiphany.

Suspension; the possibility of redemption, and also a finality. Fear and hope. What is this hanging above us? These mighty wings. Will they mean oblivion or rapture?

Louis, Cohn, and others, curse and run, anything to avoid the angel's moment. Running from themselves?

Does each human have his or her own angel? The angel we see, is this Prior's guardian? If so, is this the end version of the angel within each person at birth? Is this personal redemption? The angel, so long estranged, returning with a vengeance; an angel of doom which, yet, is also the angel of redemption.

The angel's return.

The Great Work beginning. The Work of transformation. For Prior, shifting from flesh into nothing, or can one say, into Spirit? For American society, for the world, a parallel physical transformation, but also, possibly, a transformation into social tolerance and compassion.

The great wheel turning. The arrivals and departures of the angel, of the angels. Each human, in moments of transcendence. Redeemed, not by disease, but by an acceptance of disease, the non-judgement of disease, and so, a compassion that places each being in nature.

The promised voice, the beautiful voice of the angel, whispering to us in moments of despair. Whispering us toward the day of decisions, a hard day, a day of clarity, but also the day of the dove. The spirit awakened in each being, the flesh animated.

The Great Work is the transformation of men and women from the rigid tyranny of culture, what Traherne called custom, into the angels they all are.

So the angel plunges into a person's life. Not a symbol, nor a metaphor, but an angel. Bones, wings and ligaments. Breath, and then a voice. That's all, a divinity on earth.

Poem as Sabotage

To live out his role the politician must believe or pretend that the next revolution or piece of legislation will make a difference and that the difference is worth living and dying for. The artist, with an older sort of wisdom, knows better. Like the anarchist Bakunin, he sees that the revolution that is to bring about the dictatorship of the proletariat will only bring about the dictatorship of the ex-proletariat.

William Irwin Thompson
The Imagination of an Insurrection

1. BY NOW IT IS APPARENT TO MOST PEOPLE that the Bolsheviks hijacked the Russian Revolution from an unfocussed democratic yearning. Through superior organization and tactics, through ruthless decisiveness, they undercut, then demolished, other parties, the Cadets, the Socialists, and so on, and they disregarded the fragmented will of the majority, insisting they knew what the people really wanted but didn't yet know.

With their hijacking they short-circuited a movement and wired their own dynamic into it. Democratic political development had a few manipulated fits and starts through the twenties as the Bolsheviks had to deal with the realities of various economic and social difficulties, but, in essence, it was dead.

It's possible to see today's events in Russia as the long-delayed continuation of that democratic desire. Loosely speaking, if Gorbachev was a contemporary Stolypin, the last effective and reform-minded minister of the Tsarist regime, then, forgetting Prince Lvov for a moment, Yeltsin is Alexander Kerensky, a well-meaning, ineffective, reformer representing the hopes of a long-suffering people. And the people wait for leadership, someone with the vision to focus their fundamental needs, someone pragmatic, with will.

What interests me in those moments of transition, where there is enormous hope and potential, yet the immediate possibility of disintegration, is the role artists play. In nations like Russia this is a legitimate interest. There, poets, in particular, have always been a powerful presence.

What is the poets function with regard to the full political, cultural, social dynamic of a revolutionary time? Where do they place themselves? What is their relationship to the State? What are they to the people? Are poets the "unacknowledged legislators"? Are they something more still, something not active but eternal, a ligamentary function?

2. ALEXANDER BLOK WAS THE KEY TRANSITIONAL POET during the period of the Russian Revolution of 1917 and the subsequent Civil War. He was the last, the greatest, of the pre-World War I Symbolists. In his life and work he anticipated revolution, looked forward to necessary change. Most of the Russian poets shared this expectation. The rebellion of 1905, they knew, was unfinished. The old regime was sick and had to go.

When the revolution came, there was a time of intellectual and imaginative ferment. It didn't take long, though, before some poets began jockeying for position vis-à-vis the political momentum of the ruling Bolsheviks. A lot of these writers could be dismissed as scribblers, "nimble authors" Evgeny Zamyatin called them, but others, like Mayakovsky, had genuine poetic talent.

This was an age of categorizations, ranging from the politically incorrect Acmeists to the politically correct Futurists. Blok, although much-admired by younger poets such as the poets to be discussed here, found himself thrown aside and discarded by the revolution. His mystical concerns, his non-realistic poetic forms, were jeered during readings. He was out of time.

After one of these readings, during the year before his early death in 1922, Blok muttered backstage that he could no longer write. "All sounds have stopped. Can't you hear that there are no longer any sounds?" For him, the musical poet, there was no music. Only the revving of distant machines.

In Blok's poem, "The Twelve," a Red Patrol is moving through the falling snow of a dying city. After numerous encounters, and a growing sense that they don't know who their foe is, the twelve soldiers begin to wonder who the figure ahead is, the one with the red flag, leading them. The poem ends:

Ahead (with flag of sanguine hue) —
     Invisible within the storm,
     Immune from any bullet's harm,
Walking with laden step and gentle
In snowy, pearl-strewn mantle,
     With small, white roses garlanded —
     Jesus the Christ walks at their head.

What the hell was Christ doing leading a Red Patrol? Even Blok, when asked, couldn't explain. It just seemed poetically right.

Blok, ahead of his time, knew instinctively that the revolutionary movement in the Soviet Union was extremely similar to some aspects of early Christianity, in its messianic, apocalyptic dynamic. The soldiers were looking for a Christ/leader, yearning for the end of history. What they wanted was a final answer, a scientific version of Christianity, a unitary world-view that was absolutely correct and would lead to paradise on earth.

Among intellectuals there was a general rush to be part of the great wave. This was understandable at the time, a momentum difficult to resist. Who doesn't want paradise on earth? Who doesn't want to be on the side of revolution, so long in coming? Blok, although himself initially enthusiastic about the revolution, quickly saw the future. Broken by what he knew, by the treatment he received, he died in his early forties.

Blok's death, and the manner of it, affected poets like Akhmatova and Mandelstam. They knew things were not as they seemed. There was an uneasiness in their work. They saw the beginnings of the systematic application of terror and prison, the machine of coërcion. Nikolai Gumilyev, one of the founders of the Acmeists and Akhmatova's former husband, was executed within a month of Blok's death.

Yet, even a Mandelstam, or a Pasternak, had trouble relinquishing his hopes in the revolution:

> My brother Evgeni Yakovlevich used to say that the decisive part in the subjugation of the intelligentsia was played not by terror and bribery (though, God knows, there was enough of both), but by the word "Revolution," which none of them could bear to give up. It is a word to which whole nations have succumbed, and its force was such that one wonders why our rulers still needed prisons and capital punishment. . . .
>
> Nadezhda Mandelstam, *Hope Against Hope*

A formula for all time, to fill the emptiness, to satisfy a yearning for paradise. As in Christianity. The crucial breakthrough in history, a rending of the curtain, after which all things are answered. Moving easily, logically, from 'there is no need for further questions and answers, the answer has been given' to 'there will be no further questions, no contrary opinions; we have the truth, and no one will be allowed to fight truth; people who oppose truth must obviously be criminals or insane.'

Of course, as is always the case, truth resided with those who were in political power, those who pronounced definitions and applied them. (The Bolsheviks renaming themselves the Communist Party and becoming synonymous with the State). It's possible that the poets first knew what was coming, not by the arbitrary physical violence of the State, but by the State's appropriation of language.

Words and phrases, like "revolution," "dictatorship of the proletariat," "freedom," meant what the State said they meant. This was a State, after all, run by a party that, although it had been a minority within the larger Marxist revolutionary grouping, called itself "Bolshevik," meaning "majority." Lenin knew, in the acquisition and maintenance of political power, perception was as important as reality.

(This is the crux of what happened in the Soviet Union for seventy years. Party stalwarts, for example, praised Stalin at the moment of their executions, knowing he was their killer. Astonishing events.

Intelligent people chose to believe the lie of manipulated language, giving their lives for the perception. The party, by definition, held all truth, and the party, through its leader, said they must die. Their deaths were right.)

For Blok, sound was gone. He was the first to recognize fully that this was an era antithetical to poetry. It was an era of propaganda in language.

Gumilyev was executed, without formal trial, by the State for taking part in some mysterious anti-government plot that no one has been able to trace.

Mayakovsky, highly-regarded by fellow poets initially, handed the State his gift, his vocation as poet. Wanting paradise, he embraced the lie of the revolution, and it ate him. In 1930 he committed suicide.

As had Esenin some years earlier, for other reasons of despair.

3. AGAINST THIS BACKDROP THE FOUR CRUCIAL POETS of twentieth century Russian literature: Anna Akhmatova, Osip Mandelstam, Boris Pasternak, and Marina Tsvetaeva. All four were considered important poets at the time and, through the years, their importance has been magnified.

These are the poets who, though all wavered in one way or another in the incredible pressure and tension of the era, stood steadfastly on the poet's ground. All found the personal and poetic courage (and those two ultimately came to the same thing) to adhere to their voices, to develop their voices against the full blast of a physical, spiritual and intellectual tyranny unimaginable to most of us.

They knew each other well. Akhmatova and Mandelstam loved to get together, whenever time and the State allowed, to recite favourite lines from favourite poets. Mandelstam could be brought to tears by the sound of Akhmatova's voice.

Pasternak was possibly infatuated with Tsvetaeva in the '20s, if his letters to her are any indication; or, perhaps it was the reverse. She lived for a while in Czechoslovakia, then Paris, in absolute poverty. Both Pasternak and Tsvetaeva were enamoured of Rilke's work and corresponded with him, and to each other about him.

Tsvetaeva admired Akhmatova's work, wrote several poems for her:

> Muse of lament, you are the most beautiful of
> all muses, a crazy emanation of white night:
> and you have sent a black snow storm over all Russia.
> "Poems for Akhmatova"

Akhmatova wrote about Pasternak:

> Because he compared smoke to the Laocoon,
> And celebrated cemetery thistles. . . .
> He was rewarded with a kind of eternal childhood. . . .
> "The Poet"

Writing about Mandelstam in Voronezh, where he and his wife were exiled after he wrote a poem in which he referred to Stalin as a cockroach, his fingers as grubs:

> But in the room of the poet in disgrace,
> Fear and the Muse keep watch by turns.
> And the night comes on
> That knows no dawn.
>
> "Voronezh"

4. PASTERNAK WAS VERY MUCH MOSCOW'S SON. This was his city, and he had the confidence of one embraced by his city. Nadezhda Mandelstam suggests it was this sense of belonging that kept Pasternak so well-balanced for so long in the labyrinth of Soviet politics and literature. It was only later in his career that he came into direct conflict with the State. When he was ready.

Pasternak knew how to be careful. When Mandelstam, in the street, recited his new poem critical of Stalin, Pasternak was horrified and told Mandelstam he would pretend he had never heard the poem.

Yet, other times he risked everything with acts of bravery and generosity. While others shunned those who were arrested or exiled by the State, Pasternak was known to visit, offer moral support to the family, and leave behind money.

Hand in hand with Pasternak's diplomatic approach was a tendency toward passivity. If all his care and diplomacy helped him find his way through dangerous territories, it was his literal passivity, at times, that kept party leaders from noticing him. Often this was the best way to survive.

Pasternak's passivity went beyond the physical. All one has to do is read *Doctor Zhivago* to get a sense, in Zhivago, of Pasternak's apprehension of life as something that happens to you.

Many acquaintances commented on Pasternak's childlike character. He was a man, and poet, who loved the physical, sensuous reality of human existence in nature. Human events had cause and effect, but they were contained within the larger causality of nature.

Zhivago is curiously indecisive, moving with the flow of history, writing his poems on specific tables with specific sounds. Wolves howling outside the winter window.

In 1935, at a writers' conference in Paris, Pasternak apparently said, "You are organizing against Fascism, but it's a mistake. Don't organize. Organization of any kind can be manipulated, and it is always fatal therefore to organize. The only duty of artists is not to organize, not to be organized, to resist organization" (quoted by Peter Levi in *Boris Pasternak*).

This suspicion of organization, the potential and actual loss of poetic independence, illustrates Pasternak's philosophical stance of passivity. In this instance, not simply meaning that "life happens to you," but "life is action and organization, and it is the uncategorized spaces between actions; the poet's duty is toward poetic freedom and open-ended living."

With Tsvetaeva, the most fiery of the four, this insistence on poetic freedom was rather more aggressive than with Pasternak. In her personal life she was known for emotional extremes, for quick, impassioned love affairs. She also alienated many with her quicksilver changes.

In exile she existed somewhere between the innumerable expatriate Russian factions, never fitting in. After returning to Russia, she hung herself in a doorway in Elabuga, Tatar Socialist Republic, where she and her son had been evacuated in the face of advancing German armies.

Like Pasternak, she originally came from Moscow, but she had no need to be accepted by the city. She stormed through Moscow on her utterly individualistic path, a path that gave her much grief and loneliness. Hers was a tempestuous life, and her poetry a fire in the attic.

She had the temerity in a public reading, during the early years of the revolution, to begin reading a poem sympathetic to White soldiers in the civil war, and sympathetic to the Tsar. The chairperson of the event interrupted her reading. Freedom and revolution are rarely the same thing.

> . . . every poet's attraction to rebellion personified in one person. He who is not attracted to the transgressor is not a poet. It is only natural that under a revolutionary system this attraction for the transgressor becomes counter-revolutionary in the poet, inasmuch as the rebels themselves have become the authorities. . . .
>
> Marina Tsvetaeva, "Pushkin and Pugachov"

This is a stance that is utterly flexible and, at the same time, steadfast. It is a position that recognizes the shifts that occur in the confluence of time and idealistic action. The wheel turns, and only flexible things, like non-ideological poems, remain. At one moment the poet is considered a revolutionary, the next counter-revolutionary.

It is not the poet, not the poems, that have changed. They contain change within. Like the seasons, which perpetually remain the same through their changes. What has changed is definition, the approved language of political power (whether this is the State or a literary group). What's left today is right tomorrow. The extreme left and extreme right meet.

For Tsvetaeva, authority was authority. It didn't matter where it came from, what its intellectual rationale. Authority always behaves in certain ways. It needs to close, encage, it needs to hold in its fist. The come and go of touch, the transitory moment of contact, whether body or spirit, is a threat. Authority is never comfortable with poetry.

Poetry undermines and sabotages authority simply by existing. It resists categorization and manipulation. There is something about

Interim: Essays & Mediations

the poem, no matter how one tries to trace its roots, its influences, that eludes definition. Ultimately, it comes from nowhere and goes nowhere. A moment of process that gives voice to what is voiceless. Something powerless. And so, enduring. The poet is the one who always disappears,

> . . . the train everyone always arrives
> too late to catch

> for the path of comets
> is the path of poets: they burn without warming,
> pick without cultivating. They are: an explosion, a breaking
>   in —

> Marina Tsvetayeva, "The Poet"

6. Osip Mandelstam loved music, loved hearing it and talking about it. His muse was like some composer. His wife, and others, noted how he listened over one shoulder to the hum that only he heard. He was surprised no one else in the room could hear. It's how he wrote.

Harmony, and classicism, that was Mandelstam. He believed completely in cultural continuity. You could never originate a culture, only work out of an existing one. In his own work he built, more consciously than most poets, on what had been written before, on the cultural architecture not only of the Russian poets, but all poets he read.

Mandelstam felt keenly, despairingly, the disjuncture of his era. As if he existed between two centuries, with a violent break in continuity. Only poetry could once again connect the parts.

> . . . To wrench our age out of prison
> A flute is needed
> To connect the sections
> Of disarticulated days. . . .

> Osip Mandelstam, "My Time"

Mandelstam always insisted the poet was simply another person on the street. Each person had a place, and he was interested in how a person, an individual, fit into a functioning society.

As poet, he recognized the importance of his role in Russia. He knew he would always write; he knew, sooner or later, authority would turn its watchful eye on him, and he knew the poems would long outlast authority. When the horror became unbelievable and unrelieved, people would need the voice. To say what had been, and to unify experience.

Literally starving, moving restlessly from town to town, room to room, in his exile from Moscow, Mandelstam couldn't be published, couldn't perform a reading, wasn't even allowed to translate others to make a living (translation being the State's favourite method of keeping poets from writing their poems).

He could only keep composing, afraid to put words on paper. He made his poems by reciting them to his wife, Nadezhda. She copied them out, then either hid them or, more frequently, memorized them and held them until a time came, two decades after Mandelstam died anonymously in some labour camp, when she could release them.

> A star can only be a star,
> Light can only be light,
> Because whispering warms us
> And babbling makes us strong.
>
> Osip Mandelstam, untitled poem

7. SOLZHENITSYN ONCE SAID THAT IF A PERSON, upon arrest by the KGB, wanted to survive spiritually, he or she must, at the very moment of arrest, sever — spiritually, physically, and psychologically — all ties with loved ones. Then the interrogators would have only the individual, with whatever courage he or she possessed, to deal with.

One had to have absolute resolve, the prisoner's resolve to survive spiritually, and to be a witness. This was the resolve of the poets who served as witnesses. They partook of the prisoner's reduced, unaccommodated condition.

Anna Akhmatova was silenced through the imprisonment of her young son Lev. To the extent that she did not publish poems, to the extent that she, like Mandelstam, belatedly tried to write a poem of praise to Stalin, hoping for her son's reprieve, the State succeeded with her.

In the end, though, she triumphed. She outlasted Stalin, dying on the thirteenth anniversary of his death. The poems she had written in her head came out. People stopped her in the street to thank her. Her poem, "Requiem," is one of the most magnificent poems of endurance, individual and national. It is a poem about one of the oldest themes known, individual human existence in the face of the awesome machinery of authority, in the context of time and earth.

Akhmatova, with more time than Mandelstam, with a clearer, earlier resolve than Pasternak, was, finally, the finest witness for her people. Both in her deep inner strength as she waited out her son's imprisonment and her own possible incarceration or execution, and in her poems speaking the times.

It was as if her privileged upbringing in the Tsar's town, Tsarskoye Selo, her natural physical beauty and elegance, her immense dignity, had prepared her for a role she recognized and accepted. In "Instead of a Preface," from "Requiem," she wrote:

In the terrible years of the Yezhov terror, I spent seventeen months in the prison lines of Leningrad. Once, someone "recognized" me. Then a woman with bluish lips standing behind me, who, of course, had never heard me called by name before, woke up from the stupor to which everyone had succumbed and whispered in my ear (everyone spoke in whispers there):
"Can you describe this?"
And I answered: "Yes, I can."
Then something that looked like a smile passed over what had once been her face.

Here's the self-knowledge, the knowledge of time. The poet's duty. She is witness to the human events of a terrible age. She is also witness to the natural world continuing everywhere. The eternal context of human activity.

Hans Magnus Enzensberger writes that poetry's "political mission is to refuse any political mission and to continue to speak for everyone about things of which no one speaks, of a tree, a stone, of that which does not exist" ("Poetry and Politics").

Akhmatova wrote of love and reeds and storms and God. Like Mandelstam, like Pasternak, like Tsvetaeva. They wrote of things outside ideology. Things which did not "exist" during the tyranny. This was their sabotage. Although each of them learned personal silence at one time or another, they emerged, in their voices, from Stalin's imposed silence.

Zamyatin, writing in 1921:

> Russian writers are accustomed to going hungry. The main reason for their silence is not lack of bread or lack of paper; the reason is far weightier, far tougher, far more ironclad. It is that true literature can exist only where it is created, not by diligent and trustworthy officials, but by madmen, hermits, heretics, dreamers, rebels and skeptics. But when a writer must be sensible and rigidly orthodox, when he must make himself useful today, when he cannot lash out at everyone, like Swift, or smile at everything, like Anatole France, there can be no bronze literature, there can be only a paper literature, a newspaper literature, which is read today, and used for wrapping soap tomorrow.
>
> Evgeny Zamyatin, "I Am Afraid"

In giving themselves to their voices, these poets, because of time and place, gave themselves to the nation, not the State. Outside the millennium of ideology.

Pasternak, shying like a horse, nervous and fine; growing clearer and stronger with age and readiness. Tsvetaeva on fire, burning out. Mandelstam, looking bravely past the shattered architecture into chaos. And Akhmatova, living out her last life with infinite patience and precision, telling us she would not return again in any form.

Something Left Behind

THE CITY IS GONE, the city I spent most of my life living in. At least it's gone in terms of what was and what is. Sitting at my computer in Vancouver, I try to put to words my experience of my home city. What is this city? I write a brief essay and read it. I recognize I have written a city that doesn't exist, though there is still a city with the same name, though this city, in the present, has roots in what I know as Winnipeg, and the Winnipeg before that.

I know, when I moved away from Winnipeg in 1996, that the heart of the city, Portage and Main, had been irretrievably altered. An intersection that had seen the riots of 1919, that had been celebrated as the geographic centre of Canada, the windiest spot in Canada, had become an underground mall. These changes, among others, I had witnessed. The death of character, of aesthetic and emotional value for the sake of commerce. I had a sense of the immigration patterns shifting, a sense of the character of most of the suburbs around the larger city. But a decade away is a lifetime.

What I know is memory, Winnipeg as memory, the Winnipeg I moved to some forty years ago. When I return, I run into something that is still there, always the wind and spring's dust, but I have lost the city as a vibrant daily reality.

I have no interest in writing a nostalgia piece. Yet, there is an urge to put into words something about that city, something I know about it, something I lived. It's in me, an inside map. It is part of who I am.

I was born an hour's drive southeast of Winnipeg, always aware of the city. Winnipeg as my point of reference. Each summer my family would drive into Winnipeg to picnic at Assiniboine Park. Tree-shadowed Wellington Crescent suddenly opening up through gates into a dazzling open field. Men in blazing white clothes played cricket beneath a July sky. We passed by. We'd walk through the zoo. I remember the mangy lions. One story had a lion pissing through the bars onto gawkers. I hoped it was true.

As I became a teenager, the city also grew. At night you could see Winnipeg's glow, a distant fire, or northern lights. I was drawn toward the shifting colours, a promise of another life, a promise of some kind of freedom. My immediate connection was via radio. Music was thriving in Winnipeg, and I wanted to be part of it.

Winnipeg had a system of community clubs. All the usual prairie sports were played throughout the year. On Friday nights the clubs held dances. A hundred garage bands sprang up. The city was crackling like a brilliant short-circuit. Sparking, animated and alive. Meanwhile, there wasn't a rock musician in sight in my town.

I'd hold the radio to my ear under a blanket; I wasn't supposed to be hearing rock 'n' roll. Peter Jackson, PJ the DJ, opened his show with Bill Haley's "Rock Around the Clock." I listened for the music, felt its current run through my body, electrifying me, but what also seeped through were the announcements of groups playing at the various community club dances. Forty miles away, I never got to go, but I imagined the gigs and the bands. A cauldron of energy and passion, and the names were magnets.

Finders Keepers, The Deverons, The Eternals, The Squires, The Mongrels, The Electric Jug and Blues Band, Chad Allan and the Expressions. "Shakin' All Over" still holds that garage band sound of unfettered joy and spontaneity, that reach and cockiness.

It was a blue-collar city of immigrants. The North End in particular. But there was also Transcona with its shunting boxcars. St. Boniface was the French section, with its dominating cathedral. After the cathedral burned in 1968, its front wall was all that was left standing. At night the stars can be seen through the blown-out rose window, like a small eternity. Louis Riel and his mother are buried a few feet away.

A city of wealthy merchants and traders but, more importantly, a city of workers. That was the Winnipeg I moved into in the mid-60s. Not nearly as radical as 1919, but still a sense of workers' grievance there, a desire for social justice. The election of Ed Schreyer's NDP government in 1970 was a shock to the business community. In their wilful ignorance, many thought communism had taken over the province. Duff Roblin, the Tory premier in the '60s, was probably as radical as the NDP in some ways.

A city built near power points in the earth. A city at the geographical centre of Canada and all of North America. A nexus. There is a compactness to Winnipeg that isn't there in larger Canadian cities, and it galvanizes, engenders an intensity I have not experienced elsewhere. A generator humming at the heart of the continent.

Beginning on Riverwood in Fort Garry, living there with my cousin Ray in one small room, and attending university. I'd write while he was out with his girlfriend. I understood in this room that I would always write, though I didn't see beyond the faint possibility of one book. That's all I wanted, one published book. It would be something. But it would take work, that I knew.

From there to Edmonton Street. This was the core of apprenticeship. Living alone with a pull-out couch, a hotplate and a window onto Central Park. Reading six hours a day, I remember the impact of images. In *A Portrait of the Artist as Young Man*, the young woman standing in water, with her skirts slightly raised and seaweed clinging to her bare leg. Thinking that I was experiencing the same thing as the fictional Stephen. Not something I could put a name to, except I knew it was better than religion; though, strangely, not far from it, in a way I didn't understand. Allowing myself to fuse feeling and thinking and free to go anywhere.

Going for long walks with images circling my excited mind. Carlton and Ellice, where Lenny Breau often played in a club, and up to Qu'appelle, Balmoral, and Cumberland. Finding there the edges of an urban First Nations community; suddenly aware of an old presence in the heart of the city. Knowing so little about it. Across Notre Dame to McDermot and back down Adelaide.

Getting back, needing to write. Writing for hours. Not sure I have ever felt such happiness. Looking up through the window, now and then, watching the old men on benches in Central Park. Taking time off for the Capitol, or the Gaiety, for a matinée. I'd sit through three or four movies in a row sometimes. And, perhaps, after some obscure movie with Gina Lollabrigida, running back to my room to catch her sensuality in a poem. Thinking it couldn't be done, and it couldn't. That must have been 1966 because I lived there during the great snow storm of March 4 of that year. Snow not only up to my window, but to the top of it. I couldn't see out.

Then, months later, it was Stradbrook, behind the fire hall, with Ralph and Ryan. Too crowded to write much, but living in tight quarters with two interesting guys was part of writing. You don't have to have a pen in your hands. Smoking Pall Mall cigarettes bought at Glow's Drug Store on Osborne.

A year later, after a month or two on McGee, writing songs with Melvin on Beverley Street. He on guitar, me on lyrics, and the two of us singing. Crazy songs, often with absurd lyrics. Sometimes I'd pound away on an empty Quaker Oats box. Terry, upstairs, coming down with his mandolin or twelve-string. God, he could play. Song working its way into my poems. Becoming aware of that and working at it. How to get the music on the page. Feeling the heat, the passion of working it out in words. Needing to get it right, the resonant image, and always the music, the rhythm of heightened all-night talk. My overheated brain and the heat of Winnipeg.

I'd feel it on River or Cauchon. Walk a few blocks to hear A Patch of Blue, a cover band, playing in the pub at Champs. When the pub closed, I'd go downstairs to the lounge with Frank, Richard, or Ralph. The music was slower there, quieter, and we could talk. Pat Riordan or the Don Brown Trio playing. With Frank it was always philosophy and literature, Camus most likely. Ralph and I were both writers, so it was poetry and fiction with us, but lots of theology as well because of our backgrounds. Richard dreamed visually, telling me what he was working on just then; often we'd head out, down snowy Stradbrook to his place on Lewis to check out his latest painting or drawing and have another few beers.

It mattered. Nietzsche or Camus. It meant everything to us. Hans Neufeld arguing Nietzsche as he drubbed me at eight-ball. Braque, Mondrian, or Modigliani. Richard showed me Kelly Clark's work, too. Kelly, a Winnipeg artist, doubled as visual artist and folksinger. I was into D. H. Lawrence, Kazantzakis, and the Russians. We dug in as if everything depended on it. And, always, a musical soundtrack behind it all. Bluesy, rocky, with a raw drive; blue-collar music. In the end it was simply about being alive in our bodies as our thinking went where it needed to go.

Some days, in the heat of blue-sky summers, bands would play at Memorial Park, its fountains jetting high into the air. Early Guess Who playing on a flat-bed trailer once. Neil Young had left by 1966, I think. Demonstrations too. 1967. I remember George Amabile, poet and prof, and singer/songwriter Jim Donahue, singing at some protest. Paddy wagons were parked on Osborne, cops waiting to arrest anyone stepping out of line, and there were a lot of lines to step over those days.

What remains of any of this? This intermingling of people, these singers and painters, the long nights of talk and drinking; these streets, this city.

As far as I can tell, it's still a city of workers and journeymen, of straight-ahead thinking and music. No pretensions. The populations have shifted; First Nations people live where Eastern Europeans used to; Eastern Europeans live where the Anglos used to, and so on. Other populations arrive now, have for years; Asians, Africans, South Americans. Each influx stirs something different into the mix. The city changes.

The musicians are there. I know only a few of them. You've just got to find the venues. You can hear the Weakerthans, sometimes sardonic, always clear-eyed without illusions. Debra Lyn Neufeld. Joanna Miller. Or the Wailin' Jennies with their harmonies, Gord Kidder weaving blues with his harp and, now and then, Righteous Ike showing up to weld a country quaver with the Delta. For pure Winnipeg dark humour, over-the-top vengeance, you just have to listen to the bluegrass D. Rangers plug in, becoming the re: Rangers, and snarl through a version of Big Dave's song "Gone." It is utterly deranged, from the lyrics, through the circus organ and out-of-kilter guitar solo, to the amazing vocal delivery by Jaxon Haldane; nothing smooth and silky there. And, when I hear Dave's voice, the Winnipeg I know is still there. He's absorbed it, his vocal cords saturated with the city, everything raw and true.

Bands still play at the Royal Albert Hotel as far as I know; there's blues at the Windsor. In the depths of the night Warkov still works ghosts into masks and paper sculptures in the North End. Miriam Toews, just down the street from Dave, sits at her computer and sends dark and funny Winnipeg and Southeastern Manitoba characters out into the world.

Richard's remained in Winnipeg, painting when he can. We talk on the phone infrequently. Frank's there, I think, but I've lost touch with him. Like me, Ralph has moved. Vic Cowie, who inspired so many with his brilliant lectures, has died, as has another great teacher, Carl Ridd. Lenny Anderson leapt from the Silverwood Dairies building long ago. Patrick O'Connell and Marvin Francis, poets, and Sheldon Oberman, story-teller and writer, have also left us in the last while. And there are others. They are ours. They've all taken something of Winnipeg away with them, something of the city I know, still know with my inner map. And something's been left behind.

Desire and Prayer: Notes on *The Shunning*

SITTING AT THE TYPER, a blank sheet before me; the finished book, published some years earlier, beside me. How to begin the process of adapting the book to a workable stage play.

It is already a play for voices. In language it's a natural for radio and, when I close my eyes, I can see it as a film; not a wide-screen landscape film, but a film of tight shots wheeling around the characters as they walk in and out of events, talking and worrying with their gods. As a stage play it is not entirely clear to me.

I need to discover what the theatrical possibilities are within what is already written. I need to see to what degree I can work my cinematic imagination into theatre. Film, I've always thought, is essentially a matter of close-ups, of understatement in acting; not so the stage. At least, not from what I know of it.

It makes me go back to what it was I was working with, what I was trying to do when I began the book in 1978. I had left home long ago. In 1978 I was at the end of another line. Teaching, after six years, had drained me, was driving me to breakdown. It was another of the prisons one puts oneself into. I think the emotions in me at the time connected with the memory of my desire to get out of the hot-house religious atmosphere of my home town. It brought back the suffocation. Not the anger or the bitterness, not even the sense of injustice, but the suffocation and claustrophobia, like a small room on a muggy day.

I was going to write a book. It would say something about Mennonites in southeastern Manitoba. This much was conscious. Inevitably, it would say as much about me as about the community, but the aim was to begin the process of writing the experience I had been born into. Previous efforts, including my first books, although touching on that experience, were more in the way of rehearsal.

I had many false starts. Mostly I wrote individual poems, thinking that eventually there would be enough for a book. There were self-conscious poems about betrayal and theology. I wrote many poems. Some good ones, some awful ones, and mainly average ones. Only occasionally did a poem seem true.

Looking at the batch I did notice that the poems overlapped each other. There was something about the experience I was writing about that led to this kind of layering. Nothing was one-dimensional; no one event, no person, stood out as separate, not fully separate. Each carried within it the past and the seeds of the future.

Desire and prayer: blood, idea, the pursuit of money. Life does not consist of separate moments; they run into each other; they leap back and forth amongst each other. Life is neither linear nor cyclical. Yet we live with strong concepts of history and time, and we explain all the nuances of our lives in terms of these concepts.

I could write a layered book. It wouldn't be a story or stories, but rather bits and pieces of what later could be seen to be story. At any one point, if events stopped, if someone died, you could look back and decide on what the story had been. We tend to look for conclusions to make sense of the process. This is what we do with history. It's also what we do with form in our writing. Even the so-called "open-ended" approach is another form a writer imposes on his work.

I have never enjoyed the sense of being an onlooker in a book. I believe in inspiration; breathing in and out; the leaping, graceful deer and so, the jump of the writer's heart as he stands in a meadow, or in his house.

Richard Hildebrandt, a friend in whose house I was working, called me downstairs one night to watch "Man Alive," a religious television program. We watched a story on the purging within the Holdeman church in my home town. The young bucks, not old or wise enough to hold their positions of responsibility in the church, were out to clean up what was, as far as any outsider could see, the narrowest, cleanest church in town.

Everywhere they looked, outside of themselves, they saw pride and corruption of purpose. Especially, they seemed to see it in people older than themselves. The spiritual violence began. People were banned and relatives and loved ones ordered to shun them. Business people were asked not to do business with those considered "non-Christian" by the church hierarchy. Otherwise their businesses would be shunned. Censorship, the heavy hand of self-righteousness, took over the church.

There was really nothing new here. Intellectually, I had known about this kind of thing. When my former neighbour appeared on the screen, a neighbour who had been a friendly, faithful Christian, and explained, with sorrow and pain in his voice, how he had been banned for pride, when his wife told how she was asked to shun her husband, and how she refused, then I knew my focal point for the work in progress.

Here were a people who had been founded on several principles, including pacifism; who had separated themselves from the world and its courts; and yet, some were imposing most violent punishments on their own brothers and sisters. Where would these banned people go for human comfort?

The community had always been tight and self-sufficient; to leave it was a wrenching experience. I hadn't been banned because I had never joined in the first place; not formally, at least. If I was shunned by anyone, and I was, well, I shunned right back. I had resources as a wilful, cocksure young man who did not believe much of what the church taught.

I WENT BACK TO THE WADS OF PAPER ON MY TABLE. I found a poem about two pages in length that had the whole story within it. A kind of overture. There were the slaughtered chickens; there was the rifle and the single shot beside the creek.

Especially the image of a man lying beside a creek, one hand in the water, one boot off, the other untied, a rifle beside his bare foot, especially this image had been with me for some time.

But the man was just a man, no one in particular. It took a few more days to come up with the character of Peter, and he came by way of Johann, his brother.

A few weeks earlier I had had trouble falling asleep, wondering how to approach this book. I hit upon the idea of an old and a new

Mennonite meeting at the graveyard. The new, the young Menno, would be sitting on a gravestone when he would hear a voice. It would be a long-buried Menno speaking from his grave. It seemed pretty far-fetched, but I got up and quickly wrote out eight or nine pages of rough poems based on conversations between these two Mennos.

I saw that the old Menno from those pages, I had called him Johann, was a natural. He had humour, self-criticism, and warmth. I liked him. I had to use him, even if I didn't use any of the poems about him. But this was not the kind of man who would be banned from his church. He was too resilient and lacked pride. Well, then, it was clear there would have to be a brother.

Things fell into place quickly, before I could write everything down. Johann would be another side of his brother Peter, a suppressed part of him. They were really two aspects of one person.

Other people came to mind. My grandfather had a twin brother. Their stories were interesting, even dramatic. There were events in their lives, though not shunning, that would make for great reading, I thought. Grandmother's death by flu at an early age, the burning of the farmhouse, and so on. A few details would have to be changed, of course, or made up.

I had events that moved toward a plot. I had characters and, all along, I had the church, my memory of it, and I had the suffocation.

You hurt people when you try to take a breath. When you refuse to be suffocated any longer. What you don't always know is that they really do believe in how they live and that not everyone is suffocated by the same things you are.

Still, you have to breathe, even if it means lashing out. This is a beginning toward freedom.

If you're lucky, you'll come to the day when you've not only gone past theology, but beyond atheism.

I have lashed out against judgement, and I have judged. I look in the mirror and, often, I see what I reject.

THE BOOK WAS WRITTEN QUICKLY. In maybe two or three weeks. I had to decide to what degree I would use German, High or Low. I decided to minimize German words, but worked a lot in Germanic speech rhythms and, sometimes, word orders. Just enough to give the flavour, and to lead in interesting Germanic directions; not enough to be ridiculous. Low German is an earthy, humorous language not readily available to seriousness or tragedy.

Language, then, was specifically chosen, with Low German in mind, with the Bible and hymns in mind. It had to be a bare, evocative language. These were simple people in terms of life-style and theology. Their experiences, at best, were evocative, with no one language to speak them.

Visually, I remembered my grandfather's farm. I had spent many hours there. I had old photos of him, of his young wife who had died many years before I was born. I knew where on that farm everything happened. I choreographed the dance of "the shunning" on his farm, rather than in a church, or on the streets of a town. The places on his farm I used had spiritual value for me. I remembered what kind of boy I was when I stood in those places, when I fished in that creek. I had built-in values. These would be transferred to my characters. Inevitably I became part of the characters through this process. This was not intended, but was a corollary.

This book is set on a farm on the outskirts of the town where I was born. It's where my father was born. My mother was born in another town. This is significant only to me. I can't make anything bigger of it. It's my field.

And yet, I can find quotes from other writers that speak my experience better than my own words. How can this be?

Yet, how can this not be?

WITH THE PLAY I AM WRITING I HAVE A FIELD; the field I am creating out of my personal experience and my place in Menno history. Yet, this is only partly right. There is another element, the storm field, where creation happens.

Hardy's novels have always resonated for me, especially *The Return of the Native*. Often life is being lived out dramatically, intensely, fatally in a field. What Hardy called a heath.

In my field I have Mennos, a small group in history, and I have a memory which I sometimes think I would like to be divested of. I'm not interested in writing a broad landscape. I want close-up. This must come first. Then, perhaps, there can be generalization.

I think I can get more personal on stage. At least, it looks that way at first. I can focus on interior lives in a more concrete way than I could in the book. It will still be characters talking, but they can open up feelings in a more naked way than a book can. I'm not sure of this. In fact, the opposite may be true.

The drama will be in the tension, the interplay of the personal, even the melodramatic, with detachment. The individual will be seen close-up, alone in his or her immediate world, circumscribed not only by society, but also by individual self-consciousness. Sometimes these characters will reach out into history or, more likely, the world will intrude on them.

Thomas Hardy, as a young man, was eating breakfast when he remembered that someone was to be hanged that morning, at 8 a.m., in a town two or three miles distant. Hardy didn't know just what the time was, but he knew it was near 8. He picked up an old telescope from another room and ran up a rise from which he could view the nearby town. Just at the moment he raised the telescope to his eye and focussed, he saw the white-clad figure drop through the trapdoor of the gallows. It shook him. He had been expecting the hanging, but somehow, it took him by surprise, the way it happened just at the instant he chose to look through his telescope. Such a sudden and violent glimpse.

Shortly after The Shunning *came out, I read from it to a Menno audience. A middle-aged man came up later and told me that his father had been banned when he, the son, was young. What he remembered about the event was how his father stood in the doorway, not letting the churchmen in, and not going out himself. Then, he remembered, when the words had been spoken, the door slammed shut. He wanted to know why I had written this shunning as taking place with the screen door open. I couldn't really say. Just that it seemed right. That I could see the men in various geometries around the open door, that I could hear mosquitoes around their heads as the event played out.*

IF PEOPLE TALKED WITH THE GRACE of feeling-thoughts, that would be a talking play I would like. Not overly poetic, not naturalistic. That's what I aim for. To some degree I worked this direction in the book. Now, I will take it further. String out the lines of poetry until they're talk. Not pub talk, but clear, conscious expression of

Interim: Essays & Mediations

what's inside a person. Some story, yes, but primarily, the slightly heightened language of an everyday personal poetry.

Peter, Helen, and Johann will be subversive in language. It won't be their actions that will be radical, but their communicated feelings, or the fact that they communicate their feelings. These will stand, straight or subtle, in the midst of the religious lingo of the community; a lingo learned, and felt, only as on-going cliché. Their language will pierce through clichés and form, sometimes by playing off form, other times disregarding it entirely. They will give new meaning to old hymns. The initial, pre-cliché poetry of the hymn, as song, must be retained.

Actors will carry the subversion even further. Who knows what they will do with the words given them. With their voices, their limbs, their faces. Who knows what the director will do, the set designer, costume designer, composer.

When I was younger, I wanted to be director, actor, the whole works. Now there is pleasure in giving something up to others to complete. Collaboration. Let them make of the words what they will. Whatever they do is right, whether or not it works.

A giving up.

My grandfather, on the day he died, said, "I guess this time I'm finished."

Recently, a Spanish bullfighter was gored in the heart. As he lay dying, he said, "That bull killed me."

I remember in high school, one of Shakespeare's characters said, as he died, "I am dying." I had to laugh.

What did I know? About dying; about words.

The play will be intimate, but not as immediate as the book. There will be the close-up, the actor alone on a bare stage with his grimaces or raised eyebrows, but the actor mediates between the words and audience. In the book there were only the words.

TODAY I WENT TO THE THEATRE, having done my work with director Kim McCaw and the dramaturge, the quietly brilliant Per Brask. I was introduced to Maggie Nagle, the actress who would play Helen.

I shook her hand and looked in her face. I asked her if she was Helen. It was a strange feeling. Just then, having seen the set, the

Patrick Friesen   73

costumes, I knew this was Helen.

I wondered if she knew all her lines. If she did, she knew more of Helen than I did. I had finished the writing some weeks ago; Helen wasn't in me any more. She was there, in this actress, in front of me.

What is it I want in a play? What can the stage, with its props and players, do? Henry Miller, in *Sexus*, has a line that partially answers my question.

"I want to see how I look in the mirror with my eyes closed."

For a moment this is what I felt as I met the actress. This is something I can't do with writing. There, whenever I look in the mirror, my eyes are open.

A Handful of Water

WHAT TO SAY ABOUT *poetic knowing* or, rather, how to say it, whether to say it? Writing about it a kind of voyeurism.

"I like to watch."

Isolation.

Poetic knowing as a subject of inquiry, the apparent domain of critical writing, particularly the latest version. A procession of limousines with one-way windows.

My clear bias. What I know for myself. The knowing can't be known without the knowing. Circular. So, why bother?

Poetic knowing as sabotage.

What the hell, let's go.

An approach, not necessarily consistent. In fact, not. To iron out inconsistencies, to make a seamless theory, is to enter a wholly different activity, and to alter intentions.

This is not a study of artifacts. This is an accumulation of intuitions, observations, experiences.

A looking back and forth. In two worlds, knowing two contraries at once. And so on.

The uniqueness in everything. A kind of identification with, a kind of love. Love of the specific, in matter. Spirit suffused in matter, not separate, not inhabiting. The physical object alive, not merely technically, not as a vessel, but shot through with light. Not a lamp carrying oil, but a wick on fire. No fire without matter.

Where does that take us?

Poetry written in gestation. Not only trusting gestation, but allowing it its full time in an impatient world where many believe a poem can be written anytime, by anyone, if only the correct tricks are learned.

Right. And I can play like Glenn Gould. Just a few more lessons. Maybe I'll be a surgeon. Or, a slick second baseman turning a double play.

Give me some ideas. I'll build a poem. What's going these days?

What the hell.

Making culture. A busy emptiness. A cough behind the door.

Auden wrote that "poetry makes nothing happen . . . it survives, / A way of happening, a mouth." Add "an ear" and say that poetry is what happens between mouth and ear. The emphasis always on "a way." Something ultimately without beginning or end. Electricity, not necessarily in its effect or its origin, but in its dangerous hum and flow.

Remembering the vibrating hum of a power line in the still winter twilight crossing grandfather's farm.

Not simply what a poet has written, nor what someone has read or heard. A fusion of both. It is what happens between. From mouth to ear. This seems quite obvious.

For now, though, the question: what kind of knowing is it on the poet's end? The tongue.

For me, poetry is always knowing, never knowledge. It's process, and if you happen to end up with what appears to be a complete poem, a unit of language, image, rhythm, and content that is not completely arbitrary or studied or clever, then you have something rare. Something to be admired and loved.

Nevertheless, not necessarily something to be emulated. Not something to attempt to achieve each time because in the determination to achieve the "complete poem / artifact," the process may well be forgotten, perhaps short-circuited. Pursuit of the poem as cultural object.

Where's this going?

It's interesting to leaf through the collected poems of Anna Akhmatova. One notices how many of the poems are fragments. Out of the necessity of her time and place. She, working with snatches of verse, caught images, rags of rhythm. Not the luxury of time or freedom to make them whole. Yet the cumulative effect of a whole poetic vision, a growing, alive voice that never freezes.

Sometimes an image in one short fragment reappears in twenty pages later. As if the image echoed for Akhmatova ove siderable period of time but never found its one perfect context, never found the other words it needed. Yet the image exists on its own terms. It has to be. The fact that it exists in two or more contexts makes it its own poem. You read it differently, find another side to it.

Yes, you wish maybe it had found its perfect home. Read again, and you understand that image's life, how it still holds the potency of seeking.

A way of knowing. A fragment, through force of circumstance, Ostensibly separated from its parts, yet discovering other fragments wherever it is. Making a whole impact. A moment of rhythm. An echo. To say more would be to say something quite different, quite differently. Equally valid but not what was.

The process of writing a poem. The fragments speaking. The detritus *of poetic knowing.*

The old woman who gathers bones in the desert. On her haunches over them, singing them alive.

Rhythm and the true word, words. A field of words and not. A voice. Evoking, invoking.

A radiance.

Hey, can I talk like that? Is it okay?

Where does it fit? What do we call it? Do we need a doorman to let us in?

So many ways of knowing. Who can know all? And why? I claim for poems a breadth and a depth, science and art, mathematics of the heart. A way of knowing that is music and thought, half-thought and glimmer, that is sometimes here, sometimes there, neither here nor there.

Giving voice. Evoking, invoking. Holding together loosely. Precise. Elusive. A handful of water.

For a moment you know what you hear, what you read. A moment when you have no question, when you are all questions. You don't know when you entered that moment, nor do you know when you leave. Nothing to grasp in your hand. A memory that inevitably grows false, painting its face for the street.

Poetry, in our society, in our time, a last attempt at reconnecting with who we are, finding our songs on earth. No beginning, no end, only travel. Sometimes wonderful, other times hellish. Bits and pieces. Snatches of song.

Potentially, each of us singing through the world. If we choose to remember. A stone, a tree, an emotion. Those who came before.

Perhaps, learning to write poetry is like learning to dream. There are techniques and skills but, more importantly, there must be receptivity. A condition of spirit. An opening, a patience, a letting go.

Glenn Gould at the piano, Roberto Alomar ranging to his left; these, with skills and discipline, become states of being.

Something given.

Listen, in the face of certain moments, death, let's say, or birth, love, a piece of music, or simply stillness, all theories, the complexities and labyrinths of self-circling intellectuality, fall away. Suddenly, there is only the clarity and simplicity of the newly born, the dying, the naked yearning human spirit.

There is *poetic knowing*. It can't be explained, only encountered. Other ways of knowing have their place, their function, and relationship to each other, including to *poetic knowing*, but the poem is something outside of those ways.

Poetic knowing has always woven through human history. The wheel has turned around and around. What touched the human heart and intellect a thousand years ago, a decade ago, will touch them again. What is current is ancient. There is nothing new in thought. The charisma of poetry is that it finds fresh resonances in the same old human heart and mind, the same old experiences of men and women, the same world.

Each breath one draws is new, and not.

Veritable, unverifiable truths. Nuclear fission or not. The old man walking up the dirt path toward his one memory, the house of his birth. The white curtains. A shadow there. The creek. The red-winged blackbirds.

All things fall away. What matters is known, and is sometimes apprehended in its moment of radiance.

Clearing

IT'S ALL PROCESS. The finished product may end up as one of the worst things you've ever written though the process was one of the most invigorating. You might begin with lines of poetry already set in your mind (seldom), but the poem doesn't take off; no process at all. Another night, you sit down with nothing specific at hand, and before you know it you've got something, perhaps something fine.

If you're lucky, if you enter it, you deepen your life in the process. Each time. Nothing earth-shattering, but still, small moments of shift. Something is always on the line. You work with what you know, what's given, entering into what you don't know. The poetic process is not separate from living. I don't necessarily call it art, though it is work. Why bother if your life isn't in it? Certainly a poetic "career" isn't something to pursue on its own.

During the past year I've been engaged in writing a series of pieces I call "the clearing poems." They began, simply enough, as one poem, a poem that tried to meditate upon the prairie scrap brush I grew up in. A moment of nostalgia most likely. The poem moved quickly into a specific clearing I used to spend time in when I was a child. On my grandfather's farm.

I wondered what it was about clearings that drew me. They always had drawn me. I loved being hidden in the bush, something atavistic. And clearings frightened me for some reason. I approached them carefully, the clearing's light shining among the poplars, and I stopped at the edge. Hiding behind the last few trees. Then I'd circle, still not in the clearing. Often I wouldn't enter the clearing at all. So, what was all that about, I wondered.

Animals did the same thing. I thought of the deer I had seen, a fox one time. They hesitated at the edge as well, sniffing the air. Well, an animal wasn't going to expose itself in the open unless it was pretty sure it was safe. Was this my reason as well, some instinctive memory of predators? What was the predator? Who?

It got me thinking and writing. I quickly realized one poem hardly touched on the things that came to mind as I wrote. So, another one. Not long at all before I knew that the clearing was, for me, within my terrain, a wonderful place to ask questions, mull over thoughts, remember grandfather and his two horses, imagine my father in the same clearing when he was young, and so on. I found myself writing about jazz pianist Bill Evans, particularly his song "Peace Piece." How the hell did he get from his American grave into the Manitoba clearing? Well, by way of the differing sounds of rain on various surfaces, by way of memories of my mother playing Schumann to put me to sleep when I was a child.

I heard the rain on my balcony in East Vancouver. Its sound made me think of a particular piano piece. I played the CD. That piece reminded me of another piece my mother used to play. So, I moved the Vancouver rain into a clearing in southern Manitoba. Anything can happen in a clearing, if you listen.

Jesus walked through one day. Saw him out of the corner of my eye. That caught me by surprise. It was probably a result of conversations with my companion. I didn't know what to do with Jesus in the clearing. I put him aside for a whisky-jack. Thought of my companion; she had gone to the clearing with me last year. By this time it wasn't my grandfather's, that clearing disappeared long ago, but rather a clearing on a piece of land my mother owns in southeastern Manitoba. So, a long-gone clearing, a clearing that exists, and a third clearing of the imagination, moving back and forth between the other two and heading for some other clearing perhaps.

The whisky-jack was thought on the move. Jesus returned. I wrote a long time, trying to have a conversation with him. He was, and is, an important figure in my life. The conversation was great, the poem wasn't. I stole a line or two from it for another piece; that's it. One of my brothers showed up and, though the poem is still there, I can't quite see him in it anymore. I think he became my father. That, of course, told me something I hadn't known before.

Snow came down. Often, in my imagination. I longed for snow, the sound of it under my feet. Fundamental body memory. Longing entered the poems. Longing for what? Terrain? Weather? Dead grandfather and father? God? My lover? I don't know if poem evoked memory or the other way around (always the act of sitting down and writing evokes memory, associations, images). The kind of clarity on a cold winter's night, the moon lighting up the clearing, that I've never experienced anywhere else. Prairie thinking.

Strange thing writing about the clarity of a late December night in Manitoba while the Pacific rain is falling outside my window. Dislocations and connections. I like the rain, but it speaks another language. Different from prairie rain, different from snow. The wind here is different as well. I watch and listen to the crows outside my balcony. They place me in the prairies. Yet, it could be any clearing in any bush, anywhere.

I had to get rid of some of the longing; there was too much of it. I got rid of some, probably not enough. If it's there, it's there. But, this self-conscious shaping meant I wasn't writing for myself alone. Not that I hadn't shaped right from the beginning, but something new in this shaping. No longer shaping the individual phrase or line, the poem, to catch the moment, the precise physical description, the thought/image caught, but shaping in terms of the whole, the shape of what I was beginning to think of as a "series." Moving from the motion of mind and spirit to the editing "hand" of the brain.

I've always loved recirculating images or word choices from previous work. As if the word, image, phrase, whatever, hasn't reached its fullness yet. Place it in another context. The clearing littered with used language. Lying there with the horse shit and the columbine. Recirculating? Perhaps, interweaving. The sound a little different, the picture from another angle. Layering. Returning.

The clearing I initially thought of had no water in it, though it had the skulls and bones of dead cows and horses. Another clearing, about a quarter mile away, had a small creek with fish in it. And, away from that clearing, near a small bridge grandfather had built, the creek was pretty well a slough. I moved them all into the same clearing at one point or another. The farm becoming the clearing. The terrain conflated (well, I left the house and barn at a distance).

So, doing what? Watching at an angle. Everything happening at the corner of my eye. Trying to fool the brain, that trained dog; though useful, often tyrannical and detached. The core of poetic thinking a leaping from the rut. Circling assumptions and received, narrowly examined, modes of thought; thinking through associations, at tangents, willing to think opposite, as well as anything between.

The world, my perception of it, my movement through it; world as human civilization and natural physical reality. Thinking with eyes and ears. Thinking with my hands. A way of thinking. Earth, with intimations.

The Dog Outside the Dream

BROKEN OUT OF THE CORE OF SLEEP by a dog's deep barking, he was instantly awake; he was aware of an image melting quickly away, an image of a dog, or wolf, standing in a field, gazing at him. He tried to hold on to this, wondering if it was a dream he had been drawn out of, or simply an image that arrived when he heard a dog barking down the street.

A dog in a field. Something primitive about it, at least for the few seconds the image remained. A dog, and a sense of danger. Was it danger from the dog, or a danger facing the dog? Death, he thought, something to do with death, or a death. Where was the dog standing? Had there been trees, or a building, perhaps, nearby? He thought a building, but already he felt he was adding details. Strange to be on the cusp like this, turning between where he'd just been and what he was already creating.

A man and a dog. A boy, actually. Or both. An immense aloneness, his aloneness, the dreamer's yearning. This he felt, and he knew it came from the dream. Even as the dream disappeared; in fact, all that was left now was the idea of a dog, not a dog itself, the loneliness from the dream. He didn't doubt that. And, he now understood that he would remember that he had dreamed a dog, though no picture remained in his memory.

He propped himself up on an elbow, snapped on the light, and tried to read the time on the alarm clock without putting on his glasses. The lamp's chain still moved, his eyes getting used to the sudden light. He thought he'd probably been awake for no more than two or three seconds. There was no barking through the window now, just the soft rustling of rain on leaves. Had the barking been inside the dream? Had a dog actually barked outside the window? For a moment he thought of one dog calling the other, but the thought drifted away.

Why did he yearn? Had he witnessed it? He had been in the dream, it was his dream, but had he been in it as a character, a participant? Even the longing was dissipating.

He wondered, now more widely awake, was it possible to not be having your own dream? Could you dream someone else's dream? Well, no. If you dreamed, it was yours, no? By definition. He tried to remember the thought from a moment before, it had been interesting, but he couldn't bring it back. It nagged him for a moment. He realized if he didn't go back to sleep immediately, he might not at all.

He switched off the light and lay back. Eyes closed, he tried to empty his mind. Was it his dream, or his residual memory of it, that occupied him, even as he resisted thinking? Was it the ideas cropping up now that drove him farther from sleep? His legs began itching. He knew this itch, and he didn't bother scratching. Once he began scratching, it was endless, and he'd draw blood. He remembered the thought he'd had; the notion that a dog not far from his window had barked in reaction to the dog barking in the dream. Perhaps this was reversed. Was one of the dogs a thousand years old, or older?

He sat up. There was not going to be sleep any time soon. He felt a vague sadness, but he didn't know where it came from, nor whom he was directing it to, or should have been directing it to. Was it purely his own sadness? Well, one way or another, it was. It sat in him, his legs off the side of the bed, his hands holding up his head. He carried the sadness, wherever it came from. It was going to be his sad night. He stood, opened the curtains and looked up and down the street. Drizzle, almost a mist by now. Not a soul.

In the kitchen he poured water into a sauce pan, and turned up the element; then he reached for his favourite pale blue mug. He squeezed in some honey, then sat down on the couch in the living area. It was a one-bedroom apartment, not many steps from sleep to kitchen to the couch.

Interim: Essays & Mediations

He wondered, sometimes, about his life in this space he lived in. He'd been alone for nine years. At first the apartment had simply been the relief of his own place. He loved solitude. It took some years before he began feeling like an older man. Old, in the sense of emerging quirks. He talked to himself fairly often. Not making decisions, or anything useful like that. Rather, stupid little conversations about things like putting down a book and getting up to prepare food.

"That's how it goes. Ah, the knee again. Tea? Yes, tea, but which one? How about a change, green tea; they say it's good for you . . . and honey this time, or sugar?" And he'd hum a song, a snatch of it.

And he was quite aware of his inconsequential talk, took some mild humour from it. Sometimes he wondered if it was advancing like a disease, and he'd become one of those men on the streets who walked alone having loud, often angry, conversations with an invisibility beside them.

Probably, he thought, this talking to self is inevitable when you live alone for a length of time. Not much social life; he went days without conversations. Greetings to Fortunato, the cheese man, certainly, but not much more. Human as suppressed social animal.

There was an aftertaste of loneliness. The water came to a boil as he became aware of his sharpened senses. He was noticing details, physical moments even as they passed. And he associated them with each other. The sound of the water from the boil, and that whispering sound of rain in the leaves. When he opened a pop bottle for a quick sugar dose, he noticed a momentary wisp of smoke rising. He liked to think it was smoke, but he knew it was some other scientific phenomenon. No, he knew it was smoke, and it was the smoke of yearning. It had been released. Intangible, except for that momentary swirl. This he knew. He carried it.

His work for this night, he thought, and he turned on the computer. He remembered his friend Ralph, who had told, in finest detail, the dreams he had each night. He had enjoyed Ralph telling some of them, but others brought a glazed look to his eyes. Only the details of one's own dreams retain one's total interest. Ralph wrote his down precisely, and he did it to this day. He believed Ralph could direct his dreams to some degree. An amazing dreamer.

He wasn't going to do that, had never done it, couldn't do it. He took what he could, even if it was a single image, or possibly a sound, and he built on that. It was the raw material for his work. He had no illusions that he was recording his dreams, or being true to them. What he did was flat-out betrayal. The dreams were fodder, not much more. Was this perhaps another kind of dreaming? What can you do with the fact of a dog, no longer seen, and an aftertaste of a miserable longing?

The Dance Floor (Apparitions)

I CAME BY DANCE NATURALLY. Dance as rhythm. Earth spinning through a universe, moving through its weathers, flourishing, or holding its breath. Visible rhythms, illuminations.

Inner versions as well, parallel rhythms; rhythm like marrow, a code locked in blood. Each living thing a small world.

Dance as gesture. A foot in time. An arm. A facial expression, the tilt of the head. Hair blazing through light and space.

Dance as ritual, meaning not simply the accumulation of gestures, but their organization into meaningful patterns.

Comprehending the invisible through the visible. Seems to me this is what art does when it's not busy being art. And nothing comes closer than dance. It must have been first. Animals had dance. Certainly early humans without written words and only rudimentary visual arts had dance. Often complex dance. And they had religion.

The two were probably synonymous. Religions took place on the dance floor. Around a stone or fire. The first tangible apprehension of the human spirit in relation to earth and sky. An attempt to understand what being alive meant.

Religious dance was still here recently, say in the last several thousand years, when religion began to be named. Hindus danced. The Children of Israel often celebrated with dance. Within Islam there were whirling dervishes.

Then, in most religions, dance died. Physical comprehension of the world, visible and invisible, was rejected. Spiritual life became something abstract and, frequently, arid. Something opposed to our deepest humanity. As if we could achieve spirituality by binding our bodies and so, also, diminishing our unmediated sensual appreciation and understanding of the world. As if we weren't spirits to begin with.

Where I was born, I was warned about rock 'n' roll and dance. Both were forbidden. "Jungle music," they said, "and dance . . . well, it can take you anywhere." When everyone left the house, I cranked up my small phonograph and danced like mad. I banged off walls, pictures flying from their hooks, and the needle skipping across the record. Those old 45s.

Getting out of myself. So to speak. And into myself. Taking me anywhere.

The sixteenth-century Anabaptist, Pilgram Marpeck, said, "We comprehend the invisible through the visible." I never knew how far to take that. It might mean, simply, an acceptance of the material world as a signifier of the spiritual reality behind it. It was, at least, a recognition that there is a vital conversation between flesh and spirit.

Dance goes further. The body is not simply a conduit toward the invisible. Movement is not one-way from a lesser to a great reality. It goes both ways, and the realities are equal, inseparable.

In dance the dove descends.

One could say the dancer moves through the curtain and makes the other world apparent. The apparition, the appearance, of what we know but cannot express. The dancer moves back and forth. Until we know the other world is this world. This world is other.

All movement, leaf, animal or human, is interesting. It is more when the choreographer, like the poet with words, chooses specific movements and attitudes from within a larger vocabulary and fashions a kind of code with tremendously evocative power.

Dance is code, a precise, condensed knowing. We see ourselves in the dance. Seeing, without thought, our lost gestures. Not only what vanished when dance was abandoned by religion, but the gestures of life outside history. Doesn't matter what you call it. Life in the womb, previous incarnations, the universal unconscious. Whatever.

All I know is that when I experience dance, even as an observer, I am reattached momentarily to something old and resonant. Something nudging memory. A redemption, I guess. A glimpse of lost gestures. What it has always meant to be fully human in this place, passing through the curtain.

Dance is what we begin with. One foot in front of the other. A leap in the dark. The most we can work for, always, is a glimpse. What we call modern dance, I remember it from long ago. When I collided with the walls. And before.

Poetry and Loss

In memory of Duna Levy
17 February 1915 – 6 March 2004

FOR ME, POETRY COMES OUT OF ALL OF ME. Yes, it is a mental activity; it is, equally, an act of the body.

It was pointed out to me once that my face was ruddy when I came out of a few hours of work in my writing room. I didn't know. I looked in the mirror; it was true. I attributed it to increased blood flow. I believe there is scientific justification for thinking that.

I thought, then, as well, that I often wrote in lotus position, sitting on the chair, and just as often, actually crouched on my feet on the chair. I also often walk about in the writing room, then return to the seat. There is a lot of physical activity when I write.

I feel an excitement, an exhilaration, in my body when I'm thoroughly into the process of writing. I can't say, truly, that I can, at that moment, differentiate between body and mind.

What does this have to do with poetry and loss? Well, loss enters our minds and, less obviously, it enters our bodies. I can think my way through loss, through the grief that accompanies loss. That is not enough. I haven't always known this. I, still, tend to forget this.

I can write from my head, just as our voices tend to speak from our heads. Insufficient. The voice needs to lower into the body. Each cell of the body needs to let go grief. Each cell needs to know the emptiness of loss, and let it pass through, in its time. It can't be done arbitrarily.

Loss and grief are not identical. I do not grieve each loss in my life. I can grieve something I haven't lost, at least not permanently. Loss is inevitable, that's obvious. Loss is even necessary for all of us, and for the poet. I must lose myself in the writing process. It's an old notion, but I believe I must lose my life so I may gain it. Over and over again.

I need to lose preconceptions and received wisdom which I haven't experienced. For me, as a poet, this is an absolutely necessary step. How can I write poetry if I am using words to serve some preconceived cause? How can I write poetry if I am not open? How can I write poetry if I am not willing to consider, with full attention, the very opposite of what I think I believe, of what I think I am writing about?

For me, as poet and human, I need to be open to loss, even painful loss, take it in, mull it and then do what the poet does; write toward, through and past it. I may reach no conclusions. That is writing poetry, for me.

The poem doesn't ever end. It has its moments, its apparent completions. That wonderful thing, the finished, beautiful poem. Yet, five years later I may undo that poem with another. I may modify it, or I may in fact deepen it. The poem as fossil I want to avoid. I believe everything I write is one long poem, some parts working well, others not at all, but all parts of that mulling, that stubborn engagement with this astonishing, not quite believable, tool we call language, in terms of my human existence on earth.

My father died three decades ago. I am still writing about him, his death. I think about him, our relationship. His death moved not a hair in the larger world, but it changed everything for his wife and children. For me, his death, the way of his going, the man he was, was as important as the death of a president, a queen, a saint. This was loss. A loss I handled intellectually and, over time, emotionally. I am only beginning to let this loss move through the cells of my body. Physical grief, and what greater grief is there? I came out of his body, and my mother's. I loved this man in a complex way. We did not see eye to eye, primarily about religion. He didn't live long enough for us to come to a reconciliation, to recognize that, in the end, it was only our love for each other that mattered. That is a loss. I can do some things about this, even though he is long gone;

for me, one of the most important things I do is enter words, my best tool, perhaps my only one, to speak with a dead man in his grave, and to speak with a dead man alive inside my body.

I lost the shape of his forearms with his sleeves rolled up. I lost how he threw his head back when he laughed, how he would, in a jocular mood, produce a fake laugh that drove my mother crazy . I lost the sudden anger on his face confronted by his recalcitrant son. I lost the rigidity of his religious beliefs, and his integrity; it wasn't a simple thing. I lost his long, elegant feet.

I don't want to become maudlin here. Loss has a tendency to move in that direction. Loss is the new space you have within you, a space that can be filled quickly, too quickly, that can be left empty for a while, or perhaps permanently. Poets work with loss constantly. The lost word, lost phrase. The one that got away. We are not therapists; yet, I have read poems that served in that direction. Music can serve, a sculpture, all the arts, and the wisdoms of teachers through thousands of years.

I can't write on a full page. I need emptiness. I need the slack sail to get to work. I need the doldrums as much as I need fullness. Only when I empty out can I be filled. This is old, old wisdom. It's true. I've experienced it.

Poetry will not perform the full trick, but poetry is the ongoing process of entering loss, smelling it, tasting it, and saying something for the moment. Poetry, whether it's the kind that stops time, gem-like, or the kind that is always in motion, is artifice. The human impulse behind it, that spirit, is not.

Basho wrote:

Even in Kyoto —
hearing the cuckoo's cry —
I long for Kyoto

Loss even as we stand in the fullness. Time passing. Perhaps the fullness was not quite what we expected, so loss. More likely, that certain flash of knowledge, in the midst of fullness, that this will disappear. In Basho's case, he knew the sound of the cuckoo's cry, some time later, in another city, him older, would make him feel the loss of Kyoto. Memory is loss. Fullness is loss.

The Small Fire

NIJINSKY WROTE IN HIS DIARY that "no artist can deceive God." Whatever his specific meaning, I take "God" to mean a power, a presence, greater than the daily "I" we all live with. Whether one thinks this force is outside of one, or within, is a matter of choice, but makes little difference to my point. If I call myself an artist, a poet, I accept that, when I am honest with myself, I am in a process that interacts with this God. In other words art, poetry, is another human activity in exploring, understanding, comprehending human existence on this planet, and for it to work one must enter the process as purely as possible, with as much integrity and wakefulness as possible. I take poetry to be a spiritual activity. Even when a poet writes politically, there is a spiritual, emotional element or the poem doesn't work. The best anti-war poems do not preach, do not explain, but rather enter and explore the human spirit in extreme circumstances.

Trends. What is a trend? Is it something that has been started arbitrarily from an ideological stance? Or is it a word we use after we recognize that certain poets in certain languages, certain cultures, seem to be exploring existence, in language, in ways that are similar, that intersect? In other words, is it an intellectual exercise, or is it an evolutionary process?

I do not know what trends there are in contemporary poetry. I mean, I have seen poems, read theories, that tell me certain poets write in particular fashions to satisfy the needs of some academic imperative. While one can learn from anything, I have little interest in such poetic trends. They come and go. On the other hand, any poet can be placed on some line of continuum, can be classified in some way, and these classifications go through stages of acceptance and rejection. Times change. They come and they go.

All children are born with what adults call "art" within them. This, essentially, means we are born with five senses, at least; a body, a mind, a spirit, and we arrive on a physical earth, and we engage with it fully. Picasso referred to the fire in the belly. Adults engage in it much less fully. In fact, as we grow older, adults take away this immediacy of artistic engagement, and call it "art," with its rules, or relegate it to hobby. Our education systems do this very well. Suddenly, what the child did instinctively, drawing with a stick in the dirt for hours, or arranging stones in patterns, becomes "art," and in come the rules and definitions and evaluations.

I remember a very early love of music and words, in particular. The sounds of words more than their meanings. Their pictures. I saw both my children engage with earth, with other people, with their inner selves, through art. My daughter in dance, my son first in drawing, then in music. In both cases they did it instinctively. Used it as a means of exploration and expression.

My daughter, at a very early age, danced out Grimm's fairy tales as they played on the record player. Later she studied dance at a school. I saw her become less interested in dance as she observed its politics. It became less a pleasure and more a duty. She quit. She engaged her eye, through photography and design. Yet, I can see in her posture, her walk, her gestures, how important motion and gesture is in her path through the world.

My son was a quiet child and explained himself with drawings. He was not much of a visual artist by adult judgement, but that's how he began. He later switched to music, and he's made his life that. That is not a hobby, nor is it easily categorized as career; it's his way of being on earth, among people. It is not an art, in that precious way; it's work.

Although, of course, one becomes an adult, the brain develops in its ways, and one, to one degree or another, theorizes, makes conscious patterns, I want to always remain attentive to these beginnings, to what drove me from the start. It's undoubtedly too complex to explain fully, but words and music, and their interrelationship, was how I was at peace with myself, was how I could begin to understand the world, and the small fire I was in that world. It was a way of being aware, attentive.

We grow theories, and we try to fit the world into them. This happens in poetry as everywhere else. It limits; possibility narrows. We become experts, and becoming expert means we acquire certain knowledge in some depth while we narrow our world, narrow our perspective. A poet must remain open.

Ted Hughes said he learned, from hunting, not to constrict his view, but to keep a kind of wide-open gaze. When he looked for something too narrowly, he usually missed it. When he kept a wide gaze, unfocused, he could see motion everywhere. He claimed, while traveling on a train, reading a book, to have seen a rabbit in the bushes alongside the track.

For me, writing poetry has meant a lifetime of finding how to write in a way that most clearly approximates my thinking and feeling process. I didn't begin with form; form emerged and, though I tried existing forms, they always felt awkward to me (meanwhile, I know poets who are freed by these same forms). Forms shifted and changed from poem to poem, though for me a certain kind of long line seemed most comfortable to my thinking. My thinking process emerged from where I was born, what I grew up with. King James Bible, hymns, rock 'n' roll, *On the Road*, etc. But, fundamentally, I think these things shaped what was already there.

Voice is part of it. High and low culture interweaving. Why differentiate? The choral voices of The Russian State Symphony Cappella in Rachmaninov's "Great Ektenia," the *fadista* Lucília do Carmo singing "Maria Madalena," John Lennon's wrenching vocal in "This Boy," Nina Simone putting a spell on me, Bill Evans's voicings on almost anything. The voice of the *Duino Elegies* or *The Revelation of St. John the Divine*, the unintended seductiveness of *Proverbs*, chapter 7. Physical voice, primarily, and metaphysical voice that suggests physical voice.

Trends? It's a word that might help explain something that has occurred. Or it's a word that points toward artificial, theoretical systematizing.

In terms of trends, what I'm interested in, today, is the overall trend of where and how poetry gets written. Karl Shapiro warned in 1960, in an essay called "What Is Not Poetry," that since WWII universities and colleges were taking over poetry, not in English classes, but in Creative Writing classes. As if the keys were there, in academia, and without those keys you could not be a poet. Or, at least, you had a tougher chance in the world of publication, distribution, and the other aspects of the writing life.

Seems to me this trend arrived later in Canada. Two editors of literary journals in England were talking about something they observed about submissions from North America. The submissions were more competent than ever, but rarely had voice. In other words, the craft of poetry was well-honed, but that was all. No voice, no experience, other than the experience of the classroom.

I am in this myself. I have taught Creative Writing for the last decade. I struggle within myself. I tell my students that I cannot make them poets, nor can the course make them poets. It can make them read better, understand intellectually how a poem is put together, but it cannot make them poets. That only happens outside the hallways of academia, that only happens inside the poet. Just possibly, one or two of them will discover, through the course, that he or she is a poet. I have seen that occur, rarely.

Poetry, I believe, is about an impulse, unfettered by trend, to touch the spark, to sing, to become, in the process, a finer human being. Poetry as the childish immediacy in apprehending earth and self. Poetry as a genuinely spiritual activity, probably opposite to institutional religion. Not necessarily finished "thoughts," but "thinking musically," as someone once put it. The mulling, wondering and changing. Finding the motion of one's own thinking, and that's rhythm. And, ultimately, an attentiveness to what the world seems to be, illusion or reality, and finding one's way in and out of that; finding one's way to what one is. The patience to do the work, the deep pleasure in that.

I value, learn, change, from the unique voices I encounter, poetically, musically, and in other ways. Voices that carry experience. Voices that hold within them struggle and awareness. At my death I will not think of trends, my place in or outside of them. In fact, I doubt I'll think about poetry at all.

The Greek poet George Seferis wrote:

I want nothing more than to speak simply, to be granted that
   grace.
Because we've loaded even our song with so much music that
   it's slowly sinking
And we've decorated our art so much that the features have
   been eaten away by gold
and it's time to say our few words because tomorrow our soul
   sets sail.

"An Old Man on the River Bank"

Empty Churches

HOW TO EVEN BEGIN. My experience of religion, of church, has been intense, has been filled with mingled experiences, with effects to last a life. While there are certain constancies in my thinking about religion, there are also ambiguities, changes from time to time, experience to experience. Possibly the central enigma of religion for me has to do with how things begin and what they become. The exercising of authority where once there was wild risk of spirit. Appropriation and externalization. This enigma will remain as long as humans walk on earth.

It's a species that troubles. The mass of it, of us, of me. The most destructive species on earth; a species able, and obviously willing, to pull down the house it lives in because it insists on seeing itself separate from earth. A cruel, greedy and ignorant species that can brutalize with the finest of slogans, with the best of intentions, and the most deeply-felt falsehoods. Yet individual people are something, though they are perfectly capable of fooling themselves and do it constantly.

I love to enter empty churches. This usually means cathedrals or temples where some care has been taken with the architecture, where there is some aesthetic knowing of how space and form move us. I love to enter churches where I don't feel the human need for some seamless belief to reside in with an absolute certainty; where the building is not an impediment, but serves as place.

I love to enter to emptiness or to a person, a silent person, a body, leaning forward in a pew. The notion that here there may be spiritual struggle. Yes, the person, in a desire for solitude. The loneliness of spirit on its own, that kind of courage. The knowing that prayer, concentrated spiritual meditation, can mostly happen in solitude, and in silence. This silence may well have something to do with God, whatever we mean by that (and I don't mean a personal God). But solitude is a person's creation, a pulling away from people, even when among them. Withdrawing from congregation in order to enter thinking on its own terms, in order to learn again how to be as a free and unique spirit on earth, apart from the dynamic of congregation and priesthood, apart from the official stories shaped and augmented through the centuries.

Empty churches. Our Lady of Guadaloupe in New Orleans. St. Mary's in Winnipeg. I always book a motel within sight of St. Mary's when I visit the city. Cathedrals in Guadalajara and Patzcuaro. Other cities. San Nicola in Trieste, all silver and shiny, where James Joyce attended, as he suggested in a letter, for the theatrics. The emptiest one was in New Orleans, just a few blocks from the French Quarter. Not a soul. The door closed behind me, and the sounds of traffic vanished. Neither the icons nor the stations on the wall touched me. That story has disintegrated for me. What comes upon me is that absence of sound which is sound. Perhaps what God left behind. I don't know; as if one could come to something there. Almost. A death there, and no grief. Sadness, yes, and clarity. And so, serenity, for a moment. As if in leaving, God announced its presence. Not announced; whispered, off-handedly. Without intention.

But the absence of God, or perhaps a sense that God had lingered there and passed on. We always seem to be examining God's spoor. Tracking it, those who have courage enough, to the edge of knowing, where words fail and matter is infused, and finding nothing but the occasional, abrupt, stupefying, understanding of everything which has nothing to do with formal religion. For a moment. This is a place many have come to. Some returned. Some stayed there. Meister Eckhart, Hans Denk, Teresa of Avila, Thomas Traherne, William Blake, D. H. Lawrence, and those are just a few names from a few paths. Inevitably many such figures ran into difficulties with church or state authority.

It's difficult to write about without resorting to catch words like "nothing," "absence," and "empty." Impossible to write about and that, too, is a cliché. However, one knows what one knows when one knows; the next person may know something different. Being right, or being wrong, is irrelevant. Those are categories of thought; they are not part of the on-going motion of thinking, that process of looking at the world and always moving on. Taking in objects, but also the movement of motion. That blur. One knows when one is in solitude. Alone. One knows the pain of that, how the pain disappears when you're fully in it.

One knows when a space is empty. One knows when someone has just left, leaving absence behind, like a scent. I know this in an empty church. Yet, I don't know that kind of emptiness at all. Well, there are times I think I've grasped it, but it always slips away. It slips away because I can't know it; I can only sit near it, perhaps within it, inhale it, and say it, saying it approximately. The saying emerging out of an incapacity, out of the need to have been there.

I stop. I think the human carnival is, perhaps, at its most pitiful in church. The tearing of flesh that goes on there, the narrowing of mind, the crushing of spirit. Can one truly imagine Jesus pronouncing from behind a pulpit, or walking heavily with vestments and gems? In an empty church I can wonder, and I can smell the danger in me, that necessary danger. The smoke that suggests fire. The divinity that existed before the created God. God before God.

Once again, it's the end of April, and I'm in Winnipeg. Gerry Rosenby has done my taxes with his usual humour, salty language, and nonchalant brilliance. If there's one thing a poet needs it's a great accountant (and, perhaps, that's true in reverse as well; I'll have to ask Gerry). I wander back toward the Carlton Inn. On the way I enter St. Mary's Cathedral. There are five women and one man in the sanctuary. They are all grey-haired. Five women and one man in the pews of St. Mary's. Well, one of the women is not in a pew but slowly making her way from station to station. Pausing at each, going down on one knee and praying.

I can't even begin to speak about what is going on in her. But I am aware of the space, of human need for sacred space. All theology aside, there is simply this need to find a place where the speed and consumption and noise of the world we've made is on the other side of a wall. A place where the individual spirit can be acknowledged, can pause in itself; a place where the human can enter a state of surrender to divinity, that flare inside each of us.

We build sacred spaces. Some work, some don't. Some churches need the presence of human emotion to generate any kind of spirituality; the buildings are just buildings, functional. I suspect this is a result of a Protestant distrust of the manipulative aspects of art in religion, a distrust largely justified. It is also based on a religious notion that the only reality is an outside personal God; all else is physical decay.

On the other hand, without art, and the places it can take you, often nothing's left but an aridity of rules and duty, spiritual abstraction; what's left is the denial of matter. Some churches work through their architecture. I know sacred space in the physical world primarily; some clearing, a garden, a river perhaps, a cemetery. And there are many in the world who believe in specific power lines on earth. But we have always created sacred space, not just found it. Of course, with building a sanctified space comes the hierarchy of authority, the dousing of joy. Again that old enigma.

And I think of the Convento do Carmo in Lisbon, largely destroyed by the earthquake on All Saints Day in 1755, the roof collapsing on the congregation. I read that there was a brief attempt at restoration, but this was aborted. For many years the church stood, all skeletal arches as if they could hold up the sky, broken pillars, damaged capitals from the pillars, font tanks, tombs, coats of arms, funery steles, a grinding stone, and a carved flame-like stone shape. The guide book said the church was overgrown with long grasses, weeds winding around an altar piece and feral cats lounging and stalking within. This excites me; there are such possibilities here.

It happens to be All Saints Day in 2005 when I enter the church, precisely 250 years since the devastation of Lisbon. I notice the place is now called Convento e Museu Arqueológico do Carmo, and I have to buy a ticket to enter. This tells me I won't find what I've read about. And, of course, the church, roofless still, is not overgrown; in fact, the grass is carefully kept. There are no weeds, and there are no cats. What has been done is what we do all the time. The ruined church, decimated by natural force, has become a monument, a museum. We always seem to exaggerate and, thus, diminish things. This might have been the perfect church for me. That coming together of human structure and natural destruction and growth. It could have been a sacred place, a place of human art and aspiration fused with relentless nature; how better to come to a whole sense of what God might mean?

It is on this same journey, in Granada, that for the first time I do not enter a church in a city that is new to me. I may well have come to an end of churches. I see the outside of numerous churches and, at three of them, I witness either the beginnings or endings of weddings. At one church, located just where the Darro River moves underground because it was paved over in the early 20th century, I am struck by the beautiful dark-haired Spanish bride in white satin making her way up stone steps toward the priest standing in the doorway. They exchange a few words. Then she, in that dazzling white, disappears into the blackness of the tall doorway. I haven't bothered to note the name of the church, though I know it's along-side the Paseo de los Tristes. This hasn't been thought out carefully by me, but in a city resonating with the sound of water everywhere, with courtyards of shrubs, trees, flowers, birds and fountains, why would I want to enter a church? There is enough sacred space with-out, much of it Moorish space. Several hundred years ago, this was civilization at its finest; the harmony of Jews, Moors and Christians. The Christians, inevitably, drove the others out. Once again, this had nothing to do with spirituality.

Meanwhile, at St. Mary's, a sixth woman enters, dips her fingers in a font of holy water. Then she walks over to a marble pietá. She reaches out to caress Jesus' legs. I wonder what she feels, physically and spiritually. The smooth, cool marble, does it warm to her hands? Or, do Jesus' legs remain cool as death. I assume this is not art she is admiring, or even being transformed by. Yet, it is art and, as I look around, I see much art. Architecture, sculpture, glass work. It is silent just now, but during mass there will be music, both vocal and instrumental. Sometimes the delicate resonance of a bell. The sound in itself and for itself, outside all belief.

Mozart's "Ave verum corpus" moves me very time I hear it. This hasn't anything to do with theology for me, and I'm not sure it did for Mozart either. A sound, an image, evokes a sound or image in-side me, and for a moment I connect, and something moves in me. There is as much secular music that has the same effect. Experience, not belief.

Is this woman's belief, as she touches the statue, narrative? Or, the other woman, moving through the stations of the cross, is she immersed in the story she has received? Or, is she thinking about belief in an abstract way? Is it belief in the belief that all these things actually happened? I know the fictions of history, the cobbled-together fiction of the gospels. Almost always, it was oral poetry and riddle that became more and more prosaic, written down as law. Perhaps fiction is more powerful than history, for a while, and fiction made history is powerful indeed. I'm not sure, in the end, there's a difference. Human spiritual aspiration, the object, the space, and story. That need, and all the things that have happened within that need. Wars, beheadings and burnings, self-righteousness, hypocrisy and wrath, and sometimes love, compassion and transcendence.

I want none of the fiction as theology or duty. I'll take it for what it is. I am a naked human being first; all else follows, for all the usual reasons; and I am naked, again, in the end. Always there is the need for a ground, where spirit is not hidden but heard if we listen with attention. Whether tears or laughter, a hand in the water; the human body on earth. Becoming free of the weight of a God we've made and living unafraid, willing to be uncertain.

Snow in Trieste

THE HEAT WAS ALMOST UNBEARABLE, especially at night in the airless hotel room, a room somewhere in the centre of the building with windows that opened to an air shaft. The newspaper said it had not been that hot in Italy in a century. The days were better than the nights. At least air moved outside, cooling one's skin a little. If you sat quietly beneath an awning outside a bar, slowly sipping your rum, you were almost cool. At 8 o'clock each night, Eve and I enjoyed a meal at Al Baratollo in a breeze beside the Canal Grande.

At the James Joyce Bar the owner joined me, wondering why I didn't eat any of the food he offered but just drank rum. "You love to drink more than eat," he said. I nodded, with a laugh. And he laughed. Nevertheless he fed me a bowl of olives, carrot sticks, small ham sandwiches. "A balanced meal," I suggested.

Sitting still in the heat, I asked him about winter in Trieste. I guessed it could be severe: Trieste was known for its winds. "There is no snow in Trieste," he said, "no snow. None in twelve years. Not to speak of." It had to do with climate change, he said. He shrugged, asked if he could bring me another drink and went inside.

Snow. It was what I missed most about my home territory, southeastern Manitoba. That part of Canada where the prairie ended in scrub brush, and where the shield rose into Ontario. I remembered when there had been more snow. When I was eight or nine, and a snow bank might be high enough for me to climb it and step onto the roof of our house. I remembered struggling through deep drifts just outside town as I checked my trapline of rabbit snares. Knee-deep in most places, and often I sank to my waist. I remembered shovelled paths with walls up to my chest, paths that remained for months.

The different textures of snow depended, primarily, on temperature. Snow with a crust that you tried not to break through. You could move more swiftly if you willed your centre of gravity into a ball above your waist, drawing the weight up your legs, leaving them light and quick, and slid quickly across the crusty snow, not taking real steps. You'd break through sooner or later and stand there briefly, breathing heavily, your breath the only sound on earth at that moment. It felt as if you could feel your hot blood coursing through veins and arteries; you could hear it just beneath your skin. Like you were a spacecraft, its fuel pumping away, its exhaust playing on the snow, and you warm inside the blood and bone and flesh of body.

Sometimes, when the wind whipped up, snow swirled on the sidewalk. It was wispy, then, shifting like desert sand. If it got too bad, on the highway, you might as well park your car on the shoulder and wait it out. There was no visibility; nothing but the motion of wind and snow. Eddying one moment, loosely, then slanting hard against your windshield the next. It depended on the wind.

And, now, in this old city of the Austro-Hungarian Empire, with its ghosts and old buildings, with its echoes of Germanic and Slavic, no more snow. This city where a sauced James Joyce found his way home, trailing his hands along the buildings to help him keep his feet, but I think to find his way by the body's recognition. A city without the sounds of winter.

What changes wrought in this city? Did people notice after a few years, or are they still learning what it is to live without snow? Do their hands miss it, the hand released from a leather glove to make a quick snowball? Do their necks miss that light brush of air and flake across the neck? Do they miss the heavy walk of winter boots through snow?

When there's no snow on the windowsill, what happens to its former presence? The way it piled up at the corners of windows, trying to sift in. *Winter at the door.* That wasn't personification in Manitoba. It was wind and snow. It was a howl around the corner of the house, a whining, and a long sigh through the spruce stand.

I can't think of a greater sense of the presence of *other* than a cold, clear night with the moon lighting up the snowy field. Everything has clarity. Field, bare trees, sky and stars.

In the cold winter there is less naming of things. The earth presents itself as wind, sky, spruce and snow. Naming, from ancient times on, is the mind's identifying of earth's things. It is human consciousness. There are dead scientific names, and there are beautiful names that give us metaphors, symbols and myths, ways of ordering earth. This is how we think and live, but sometimes, it is so good to name nothing. Nor to be driven to name. Just to take a breath, visible in the air, and to allow thinking without the compulsion to categorize. Where the mind becomes wintry.

It was in Trieste that Joyce wrote "The Dead," one of the most beautiful short stories ever written in English. It ends after a man has experienced one of those clear momentary recognitions of mortality and love, of the fact that his wife will never love him with the fullness that she once loved a man who is now dead, with snow falling all over Ireland, settling over a bog and churchyard: "he heard the snow falling faintly through the universe and faintly falling, like the descent of their last end, upon all the living and the dead." The naming of the Bog of Allen, a churchyard with Michael Furey buried in it, then an end to names. Only snow on headstones. All names covered.

Joyce must have seen such nights in Trieste during his decade, and more, there. He must have walked through the cemetery where Leopold Bloom was buried; he must have walked the streets, leaving nothing but his footprints behind.

La nuit des fées

EVE AND I ARRIVE IN GENEVA after stops in Toronto and Frankfurt. Switzerland will be a brief visit before we take the train south for a longer stay in Italy. Eve's daughter Leigh works at the American School in Leysin, some ways up the Alps, an hour or two outside Geneva, and she picks us up at the airport.

After a harrowing drive along a narrow winding road with nothing but sheer drops on one side, we arrive in Leysin. Leigh has driven beautifully, but I'm discovering a growing caution of heights as I become older. When I was a boy I would scramble up the tallest trees with delight, spending whole days up there and, even as a teenager, I loved figuring out how to scale the walls of three or four story buildings just for the fun of it. No more.

We are ensconced in about as beautiful a room as one could wish. Leysin is built on a slope; in fact, the primary way up from Aigle, which has a train station, to Leysin is by cog train, a trip I love to take. The building is empty; it's an old hotel of four or five stories being renovated as a student residence for the school. As most of the students are gone for the summer, we are the only ones there. Our room, at the corner of the top floor, is small and clean and comfortable. A glass sliding door opens to a kind of veranda that runs the length of the building.

In front of us, across a valley, lie the Alps. It's postcard territory. On the Alpine meadows you can see cows, small at a distance, and you can hear their bells on the breeze. This is a sound that we realize is a feature of the town. At night we watch the lights of other towns in the valley come on as the sun disappears behind the mountains. Although this is the hottest summer in Europe in a century, we are comfortable at this altitude, particularly at night.

We will stay here three or four days before taking the cog train down the mountain to Aigle, and the train to Milano and on to Genoa, Levanto and, finally, Manarola. We can't believe the beauty around us, and our luck at being housed in such a fine place.

What is more difficult to believe is 8 a.m. I wake, in wonder at what I'm hearing. It may be the sound entered into my morning dream. All I know is that I wake to angelic voices. A moment later Eve wakes as well. What is this gorgeous sound greeting the day?

It takes a moment for me to understand we are hearing a Russian Orthodox choir. The deep bass, the altos emerging from the bass, and then the sopranos soaring above all. It's not loud. We discover later this choir is living two floors beneath us and the sound of their morning "warm up" travels out their sliding doors, up two floors, and into our open door.

We hear this at 8 a.m. each morning. Everyone should wake up like this. I can't imagine anything more fully human; the implicit sorrow of the Russian songs, the deep joy woven in with the longing; quite simply the harmony of human voices rising, with the full meaning of humanity, toward the sky.

On the third day, as we hear the singers leaving at the front door, heading for their buses to take them to a concert somewhere in the vicinity, we decide to have a look. We lean over the railing. To our astonishment, they are all in their late teens. Those pimply boys produce the rumble of bass? Those giggling girls sing so knowingly of loss and aspiration? Several adults, including a priest or two, chaperone them.

We think of these voices as next thing to miraculous. In the thin air of the Alps, lying in bed, seeing the sun above the mountains, the diaphanous curtains shifting in the breeze at the open glass door, and those voices entering with the breeze. There is a serenity to the beginning of each day, an awareness of what we are on earth.

On the appointed day we depart for Italy, but we return, nine or ten days later, for a last night in Leysin before flying back to Canada. What happens that last night is another side of miraculous. Rather, a bit of dark magic. It happens to be *La nuit des fées*, the night of the faëries. When Leigh tells us there will be celebrations and street

Interim: Essays & Mediations

parties in Leysin, I don't think much about it. I should have. It's a midsummer night's dream ahead of us.

Our hotel sits above Leysin. It's a steep descent, by steps, into the town. It's an even steeper ascent, returning. Leigh's apartment is about halfway between our room and the town proper. We go to her place, stand outside the building and gaze down at the town. We can see bright lights, hear loud music in one particular area. We decide to go there for a drink.

Well, it takes us two hours to find this place which is only a fifteen minute walk away. Each time we round a building, thinking we'll come upon the scene, there's nothing but darkness. We retrace our steps, try another route. Up and down. Nothing anywhere. Later, we realize, we actually end up a mile away from the street party at one point. What's going on?

We can no longer see the lights or hear the music. The town is quiet. It doesn't matter which streets we take, which turns; nothing. It is eerie. So far, I'm just thinking we're all bad at directions, and it is night time, so it's not too surprising. But Leigh, who has lived there for many months, is puzzled. She knows this town.

All this time we are either jarring down steps or clambering up them. I have a bad knee; it's getting worse and, with it, my state of mind. Anger isn't the word; irritated is. I want nothing more than to sit down, order a dark rum and watch people dancing.

We finally come upon the lights and the music. Eve and Leigh, seemingly with much more energy, and certainly better knees, are quite happy and melt into the crowd. I find the nearest bar, order a rum and sit down. When I get up to buy a second rum a few minutes later the price has doubled. Why? No explanation. It's at this point that I suspect I'm caught up in something that I have no control over. The man beside me orders the same drink, and he is charged the lesser price. Is it because I'm a foreigner? It could be, but the man who has just ordered the drink is also a foreigner. There are a lot of non-Swiss in this town, and the main hub of economic activity seems to be the American School, whose students come from all over the world.

I leave the bar and come upon Leigh and Eve. I say, quite simply, that I've got to get to the room. I've had it for the night. Eve says she'll walk up with me, then return. Today I still don't know what happened over the next hour or so, never mind what had already been going on.

In seven years, Eve and I have never had a serious argument; momentary exasperations yes, battles no. Once, in New York City, both of us exhausted after hours of walking in August heat, we disagreed about what we wanted to do next. We were leaning against a stone wall at Central Park near the Dakota, and discussed options. Eve walked off to check out a nearby museum, and I realized by the way she walked away she was upset. I was too stupid to know we had been skirmishing; me, in my heat exhaustion, nettled and wanting to do nothing but sit and watch people, I had obviously sounded annoyed; she, as always, was curious about the next possibility. When she returned, it was all forgotten. I had had a talk with myself, and she had found an amazing show of photographs at the museum, and that's where we went. Later that night, in our room in Brooklyn, Eve turned to me and asked, "Was that our first argument?"

Now, walking up the infernal stairs, my irritation at the way things have gone shows up, not so much in what I say, but in the tone of my voice. We argue about something; I think about the key. A pouting boy, I limp ahead of her. After a few minutes, I realize this is silly and slow down to wait for Eve. She is sad. Silently we walk together to the building. We have been assigned a different room from the one we had earlier.

It is dark, we fumble with the key, and once we get into the room, find two cots, both without sheets, and the dank smell of renovation. Nothing like the airy room we had earlier. We sit on the edges of our cots, utterly depressed. Slowly, we begin talking. What is going on this night? What was I doing? Why were we arguing? About what? We ease into each other as we talk. I feel darkness fall away from me. We talk about love.

We decide there is no way in hell we will stay in that inhospitable room, and we head down the mountainside to sleep in Leigh's extra bed. The story is more or less over at this point, except for the fact that it takes us another hour, at least, to find Leigh, and her key, to let us into her apartment. But by then I am too exhausted, in all ways, to care anymore.

In the morning we wake to the sight of the Alps and a brilliant blue sky. One wall is all window. We talk quietly. Eve asks, "You remember what night it was last night?" Well, yes, I know it was some ancient holiday that is still being carried on, more or less for an excuse to party on the street. "It was *La nuit des fées*," she says. And it all makes sense. I think of Shakespeare's play. Eve thinks of her mother's talk of faëries. Duna was born, and grew up, on the Isle of Wight. Faëries were part of her culture. Eve tells me that Duna never claimed to have seen faëries, but she always pointed out the places in her backyard in North Vancouver where they lived.

Well, we'd been had by faëries, mischievous, dark little faëries. They'd kept us from finding the street party, leading us on a merry chase for miles and miles through the streets. They'd nudged Eve and I into our small argument. How? I guess they had just brought out our darker selves. Mine, at any rate; my gall, my little spoiled act. With Eve, they brought out the deep sadness she holds inside. And the two met on the sharp inclines of dark steps in a black night.

And, like the play, all ends well. Lessons learned. New understandings. For both of us I think, a kind of possession; something that won't leave us, some knowledge we have experienced directly. Nothing immense; just some mischief, a mischief that children know as they hide from each other in the late evening, crouching in the shrubs, shivering in their hiding places. Something very old drawn out of us, something quite uncivilized, something on the other side of the haunting Russian voices raising their burden in song.

Whistling

LISTENING THE OTHER DAY to the newly-released John Lennon CD, *Acoustic*, hearing him play guitar and whistle a whole song, a demo, no words, no singing, I suddenly realized my childhood had been filled with whistling. Not my own, I was a very poor whistler, but that of boys and men around me. Women seemed not to whistle where I grew up; I can't remember it anyway. I once heard it was a sin, though I couldn't imagine why; yet I know there are places on earth where women are not allowed to sing; one just wants to be quit of it all. But men whistled where I grew up.

My father whistled in the garden, planting on his knees; he whistled while he was building a birdhouse in the backyard; in fact, he whistled just walking down the sidewalk, coming home from work. This wasn't unique. A lot of men whistled in my town, on my street. Hell, people whistled while sitting in the outhouse.

I remember trying to learn to whistle. Seemed to come an age where you just had to learn. It went along with picking just the right blade of long grass, holding it to your mouth and whistling around it as if it was a reed in a saxophone. All the guys whistled, spent time perfecting it, comparing whistles. You could whistle just to get someone's attention, or to be cool when a girl walked by. That whistle of male appraisal. And the good whistlers soon learned to whistle simple tunes and, eventually, more complex songs. Hymns, sometimes, where I lived. Pop songs, or Gillette's ads. Remembering Robert Mitchum whistling part of a hymn in *The Night of the Hunter*. That was frightening. The deliberate, relentless stalker, whistling a hymn. That contrast of blithe sound with calm, brutal intent. And, of course, the "up yours" whistling of the "Colonel Bogie March" by the British prisoners in the classic *Bridge on the River Kwai*. Whistling as code, as bravado and unity. I found group whistling unusual though; for me, it was an individual sound.

I tried to whistle. I got the odd piercing note out, more or less accidentally, but nothing coming close to a tune. I couldn't whistle at all by blowing out, only by sucking air in over my lips. And it was pitiful. Almost a matter of not becoming a man. I was self-conscious about it, then just dropped the whole idea, and forgot about it. Until now.

No one whistles. Not in the city, not down the street I walk along. I don't see men walk to work, whistling. On construction sites, no whistling. No music at all, unless it's crappy pop music from a transistor. Wait a minute, no one has transistors. You might see earphones; CDs playing on Discmen, sound leaking out as you walk by. Obnoxious cars vibrating with bass speakers. A barrage of sound.

What happened to whistling? That kind of quiet pleasure. The nonchalance of it, its lightness. It's hard to be down when you whistle. Is it a simple matter of the joy having gone out of life? No one wants to get to work, no one wants to be doing whatever it is they're doing? Or, is it the city? Too loud, a whistle can't be heard, not even by the whistler? I've read of a bird that has changed the pitch of its mating whistle because its old one could no longer be heard in the noise of the city. A matter of survival.

My youth was filled with whistling. Singing, too; singing in public, for the pleasure of it, or expressing the day's happiness. Women seemed to do that more than men. Mother hanging up the wash on the line, always singing; a Scottish ballad or a hymn. I hear someone whistle or sing on the sidewalk now, on Commercial Drive, and I think they're goners.

When I stop to think about it, it occurs to me that, perhaps like the threatened bird, we could be going extinct because we don't whistle anymore. Not in touch with what whistling means. Something important missing. Breath shaped by the tongue and lips; the body singing without a word. Like a bird. We may be losing our physicality as well as our joy. Losing the ease and uselessness of whistling, the impulse to whistle. You may well be alone, but you're not lonely when you whistle.

Patrick Friesen   113

I go back to my CD collection and find several tunes on which Lennon whistles. "Jealous Guy," for example. A holdover from his youth, I'll bet, when he heard men whistling as they walked by, when he and his friends taught each other. Levon Helm whistles out the last Band song, "Livin' In A Dream." And, though that isn't one of their better songs, the whistling is a perfect way to walk out, nonchalantly. The whistle is a connection to boyhood, and to another time, for me. The 50s, early 60s, is when I last remember whistling as an easy, spontaneous expression of the human spirit.

It's never still enough to whistle now. A colleague asked me a few weeks ago, "doesn't anyone know how to whisper anymore?" Whispering has no pitch; it's sheer intimacy. Today, the loss of intimacy among friends, among neighbours, in the backyard, on the street. The disappearance of places in cities and large towns where you can actually whisper, where you can whistle. Places where piped-in music, television, or traffic don't overwhelm.

I don't know. Something seems gone, and I hadn't even noticed. But, you can listen, through all the noise, you can strain to hear; it's got to be there somewhere. Some kid sitting on a curb with nothing to do. A happy lover opening the door to his apartment. Maybe, listening can bring it back. Someone whistling in the dark; that echo, at dusk.

Falsetto

RIDING THE BUS HOME, after watching *Festival Express* with my son, I thought of Richard Manuel singing "I Shall Be Released" in the film. I realized it was the only song I could think of, at the moment, sung totally in falsetto. From there I thought of the songs Manuel sang falsetto on. The Band's inaugural, and I still think most brilliant, album, *Music From Big Pink*, held most of Manuel's falsetto. "Lonesome Suzie" approximates "I Shall Be Released" in vocal approach, in the voice remaining at a high range, constantly hiking into falsetto territory.

After that he still used falsetto in parts of songs, as in the ending of "The Rumour" on Stage Fright (the same song in which he sang at his lowest range), but much less. While much of the beautiful and delicate "Whispering Pines" on *The Band* was sung in falsetto, it shifted back and forth between falsetto and a normal high range. An effective weaving.

Even when not singing falsetto, Manuel often sang in his highest range. This is an uncomfortable range for most formally untrained male singers; the voice often sounds strained. Manuel had a low voice, both in singing and talking. I would guess he was a baritone, possibly bass. So, why did he choose to sing in the higher range? Why use falsetto so much, much more than almost any singer I can think of?

The Oxford Dictionary says falsetto is a diminutive, originally, of the Italian word for false. A small falseness. I think falseness in the sense of unnaturalness. It is, says the Oxford, "a method of voice production used by male singers, especially tenors, to sing notes higher than their normal range." It is "a voice or sound that is unusually high." That's the definition, the technical meaning of the word. Falsetto is much more.

Falsetto is male emotion revealed to varying degrees. It can soar, be joyful, but with Manuel it is usually male vulnerability. Falsetto may well come out of wound. It is close to a cry. It is often pain. When the falsetto breaks, when the falsetto is not the perfect high sound of singing, but an almost erratic sound, breaking between the normal male voice and the vulnerable voice, between ground-ing and transcendence, that is the most naked, the most emotional sound of all. It is precisely that break, and then the uncertainty of the voice in falsetto, that is so effective for me.

The falsetto of the singer with a normally lower voice is more effective than the falsetto of the singer who is already a tenor, and trained. Falsetto in the voice of a singer like John Lennon or Manuel is something different; there it holds the pain of longing, of loss; it is reaching for something unreachable, and in the process utter nakedness. In fact, I find their need to sing falsetto at certain points to be revealing.

This touches on an interesting matter. I don't think it can be explained logically, but I'm convinced that a singer's personality and experience can physically effect his or her voice; it's not just the delivery and artistic choices. Voice is who the person is.

Falsetto is related to, but quite different from, yodelling (which usually sounds joyful, sometimes jokey; the way Levon Helm yodels near the end of "Up On Cripple Creek," and the way Dylan, in his earlier folk stage, partly yodelled in a joking fashion, or hooted in fal-setto for the fun of it, as in "Pretty Peggy-O"; Dylan is so often ironi-cal that singing falsetto would be too naked for him, too exposed and free of masks.) Nor is it the Buddy Holly vocal hitch, utilized by so many singers in the late 50s and early 60s. That feels more like a vari-ation of vibrato. It is a hook for the listeners' emotions, but it remains a stylistic tool, not quite catching us at a deep level.

The pre-pubescent boy has a high voice when he sings. There is a clear quality here. The purity of the trained boy singer, the Vienna Boys Choir for example, doesn't touch my emotions, not at any depth. Nor would the castrati if they still existed. Nor, on the whole, do the doo wop groups. There is a cool aesthetic there, no texture, a crystal clarity, something smooth, but not a fragility. There is little struggle.

The Platters use of falsetto is beautiful and smooth. Tony Williams was one of those singers who could soar into falsetto without a real break if he wanted. But just listen to their version of "The Great Pretender," then listen to Manuel sing the same song on *Moondog Matinee*. It becomes a different song, a song of confession and yearning. Williams soars without breaking. There is some emotion in this, but Manuel reaches for the note then, when he can't go further, he throws his voice into falsetto. Just for a moment, vibrating the note before dropping down. It's a complete hook, thrown at precisely the right point in the song. The reach, the leap, and the descent. He has taken an attractive pop song, with clever pop lyrics, and made it his personal story. The emotional depth is greater.

What makes falsetto work best of all is contrast, not just the contrast from lower register to upper register of voice, but the shift from the satin of a voice to the wool. Another way of saying the effectiveness is based on tension and texture. The strain of reaching, the need to do this, and the falsetto playing off a rasp in the voice, or a gruffness. There is a spot in "The Great Pretender" where Manuel could reach for the falsetto, but just as his voice moves toward it he chooses to go to the back of his throat and wrench out the words "I'm not."

The vocally untrained boy, singing to himself as he plays, is another matter. There, too, is a vulnerability, but it is the inexperienced solitude that doesn't hold the pain of a mature man. The vocal cords have not thickened with age and experience. Although falsetto is generally considered a male aspect of singing, one can hear its qualities in Nina Simone singing "The Last Rose of Summer" and other songs.

When the singer truly goes for the falsetto, reaches beyond any formal technique he has, we encounter something "other worldly," and yet of the world in its longing and pain. Is it the child being heard for a moment? Is it this sense of the hidden, the forgotten, making its brief cry that grabs the listener? Is it innocence heard in the midst of experience? Is it the inevitable hopelessness of this?

I have six or seven versions of "I Shall Be Released" on various CDs. Two are Dylan's, the others are all by Manuel (they trade verses in the version on *The Last Waltz*). One is the original recorded in a studio, the others are live from various tours and gigs. They do different things, have different effects. Only the original and the last (Manuel playing a solo gig at a place called The Getaway in New York a few months before his death) begin with piano alone. All the other live versions have Robertson's guitar joining the piano after the first three notes.

Dylan's first version is among the tapes informally recorded at Big Pink. Dylan sings the verses straight, Manuel joins him on the choruses in falsetto. This is the original version of the song. The falsetto adds poignancy, and it's interesting to understand that, when The Band recorded this song first for release, Manuel chose to use his harmony falsetto as the primary voice of the verses as well as the choruses. Dylan's later version, beginning with guitar, is folky, happy-sounding. Manuel, brilliantly, begins with clear, sharp piano notes, almost an announcement that silences us to listen. Three repeated notes, then a falling descent of the instrumental notes, but the voice entering in falsetto and remaining there throughout.

"I Shall Be Released" is a song about a man in prison on one level, but also a piece of Platonism, with a release from illusion. In either case it's about the entrapment of the human spirit, of perception, and a yearning to get over the wall. Falsetto is an inspired vocal choice. The voice is longing, and it is constraint. The voice sounds strained; it is not natural. The song is, finally, not release; it is yearning itself, as you find in deep song.

While the first version and the one in the film *Festival Express* are probably the purest, with Manuel's voice strong and filled with conviction, I find myself strongly drawn to two other versions. In one of them (on *Before The Flood*, with Bob Dylan and The Band) you can hear Manuel's voice ragged from touring. This reinforces the constraints of the voice, the singer struggling not only to hit the falsetto, but to do it by overcoming tired vocal cords, possibly a cold. He serves the song, but it's hard, harder than it's ever been.

At The Getaway Manuel's voice is thinner, reedier, vocal cords weakened, undoubtedly, by many years of substance abuse. While this is moving when one knows something of Manuel's story, it is the pathetic side of moving. We hear a deterioration that doesn't allow him to serve the song anymore. There is chagrin; something of the failure of purpose. The fall of the singer.

And there is a version where Manuel does not sing solo falsetto. *The Last Waltz*. Dylan opens with the first verse. When Manuel comes in for the second, he sings in his natural voice, and not at his higher range. Dylan returns for a third verse, now singing at his higher range, and Manuel singing falsetto, finally, as harmony. The choruses are sung by a motley bunch of famous singers and musicians. It's California in the late 70s. There are drugs and self-indulgence to make the drunken train ride of the early 70s in *Festival Express* look positively pure. Now you've got a sing-along that has lost almost all of the song's original, spare truth. It isn't the version to remember.

For me, the ravaged voice in *Before the Flood* is as effective as the original version. It's the ravage of touring, the ravage of living, before the tip over into complete excess and loss of the spirit's wildness. When one knows some biography, the fact that Manuel sang "I Shall Be Released" at manager Albert Grossman's funeral, then himself died a month or two later and had a handful of friends gather around his wintry grave in Stratford, Ontario and sing the same song *a cappella*, the song, of course, takes on weight.

Falsetto. The male voice at its highest range. It can soar, and it sometimes does, but primarily, in the classically untrained singer, it holds constraint, the longing to be released from constraint, and the purity of childhood holding a memory of freedom. Silky smooth goes only so far; when I hear need, when I hear the reach breaking for a moment into release, then falling away again, that's when I'm emotionally held.

Memory River

TO THINK AND TALK ABOUT MEMORY IS, for me, to go back to childhood and into old age. Perhaps the question of poetry and memory
is as simple as a fusion of the child's rhyme "row, row, row your
boat gently down the stream / merrily, merrily, merrily, merrily / life
is but a dream" with Shakespeare's "We are such stuff / As dreams
are made on, and our little life / Is rounded with a sleep." Substitute
for "dream" and "dreams" the words "memory" and "memories,"
and add Basho's haiku "Even in Kyoto / hearing the cuckoo's cry / I
long for Kyoto," and you probably have the gist of my thinking.

There is no one approach to either poetry or memory, but one
function of poetry is to be a song of longing for what is not there,
nor ever was. Not longing for the memory itself, but for something
outside of memory, the absence which is the context of memory; the
state of longing in and of itself. We long for what can't be named;
the unremembered. As Basho's poem suggests, even in the present
we long for what is right before us because everything holds within
it its own disappearance and loss, its own state of non-existence,
and as we experience the present we experience it as loss.

This may well be one of the main goads to writing poetry. Memory is a trick to remind us that something may have been there, or
perhaps not. Memory is not something you can trust. So poetic
longing, like the Portuguese concept of *saudade*, is for something
that cannot be named, a home that does not exist. This is a state of
suspension that can't be resolved except, possibly, through death.
For this reason, I suspect, poetry of longing pays attention to physical detail, is awake to the material world; a shawl, a bottle in the

ditch, whatever; it's all we can claim to know, and even that claim is tenuous. The physical world is a river, and it is the boat we're on as we drift from what we don't know toward what we don't know. There is a mist. We look back. Nothing. Looking forward, also nothing. We catch glimpses of the shoreline.

About two years ago I abruptly remembered an event from my childhood. I remembered shooting an arrow in our backyard; the arrow fell into a rain barrel positioned at one of the corners of the house where a vertical pipe let water run from the eaves into the barrel. Rain water was better for washing one's hair, apparently, than the mineral-loaded local water supply.

The barrel was half full. I was probably seven or eight years old. I couldn't reach to the water level to retrieve the arrow. I hoisted myself up to the edge of the barrel and balanced at the waist, leaning into it. I still couldn't reach the arrow. I inched forward, overbalanced, and fell head-first into the barrel. My head was under water. My hands began scraping at the sides of the barrel, trying to back up. This didn't work. My hands just slipped off the sides. I remember the feeling of the sides of the barrel on my hands, a rough texture, perhaps rust. I remember the light under water. I was drowning.

Suddenly, I felt hands grasp my ankles, and next thing I knew I had been hauled out, standing, soaking, in the sun. From the kitchen window my mother had seen me tip into the barrel.

I called my mother in Manitoba, thinking I'd get her perspective on what had happened that day. I was interested. She didn't remember the event. In fact, she said, we'd never had a rain barrel at the corner of the house. I was astonished. After talking about other things, I hung up and sat there, wondering. How could I have such a strong memory while she, an adult at the time, said it had never happened. Surely an adult remembered things better than a child, especially something important like saving her child's life.

A few hours later, or perhaps it was the next day, my mother called back to say that she remembered now that we had indeed had a rain barrel at the corner of the house. However, she had not dragged me out of that barrel.

Well, a small crack of light. Her memory was not perfect. There had been a rain barrel. Or had there? Perhaps my memory had created a new memory in her. Perhaps none of this had happened. On the other hand, maybe it had. What had caused me to remember? I don't remember. But, it could have been the music I was listening to, or it could have been the quality of light on the beech trees across the street from my apartment.

Whether the event happened or not may in fact be irrelevant. Perhaps the nature of time makes all events non-events, eventually. It neither happened nor didn't happen. It's lost the way a dream is insubstantial; just something going on in the circuitry of the brain.

We have our scars. Memory etched on the body for a while. Even in a lifetime a scar can fade. I look for the scar on my hip, and I can hardly make it out. The story connected to the scar I remember, though it shifts with time. The basic facts are there, I think, but there is some frill. What does my body remember? Are memories stored in the cells of the body itself, and the brain is simply the amplifier of these memories?

I believe the body holds memory. However, I don't think it stores it any more perfectly than the brain. I may well have heard a story of some other young boy tipping into a rain barrel, and this story eventually became my story. There are other possibilities.

I don't know my future. I don't really know my past. I have stories for both, and I tend, like all of us, to believe the stories of the past. This is how I exist. I create my life out of memory. I shape and hone the memories as I move through time; not in order to fool anyone, but because that's how the story seems to work best at the moment as I try to understand my existence. I add, subtract and modify. Yes, I make memories up.

I remember reading in a book by Oliver Sachs about a man whose memory lasted only a matter of moments. He could see a friend through a window, wave to him, and seconds later, when the man rang the door bell, wonder who it might be. He had no memory of having seen him through the window. Most of us would say this is not living. We need memory to live even if that memory is partially false, totally false, or momentarily true. I exist on stories and, most importantly for me, on the poems and songs of longing.

Even in Kyoto I miss Kyoto. I can listen to a recording of *cante jondo*, a Spanish song form filled with melancholy and longing.

Interim: Essays & Mediations

Or *fado*, in Portuguese. I don't need to have a translation; I know the longing from the music, from the fabric and texture of the voice singing, from the silver ringing of the guitar. It is a longing for everything, and nothing. Simply, a state of longing. Caught in memory's truthful lie even as I float forward into something I don't know.

I prefer the word "longing" to "nostalgia." It is less specific, and that is fundamental to what I'm talking about. Nostalgia is literally a painful longing for home (Greek *nostos*, meaning "return home," plus *algos*, meaning "pain"). What I'm suggesting is that there is no home. If we're talking about some past "home," well that certainly doesn't exist. Whatever was is changed, is no more. Home is pure concept, not reality.

One cannot return in any way, so one longs into the future for the past. That's what longing is. And, as the Basho haiku suggests, each present event is already past, is not new. Our lives, like an archaeological dig, are accumulations and layers, and we are least awake to the present.

Home is only the present moment — where one is, how one is — and this present carries the seeds of its loss. Home is in the process of being awake. When one enters writing fully, for example. But, minute by minute, it disappears. There is nothing to hold onto. One sees this in Joyce's *Ulysses*, and it's no accident Joyce admired Greeks and Jews, people of diaspora. A perpetual journey on water, in the case of Ulysses, an eternal wandering on earth for the Jews.

I recently heard, on the radio, a scientist insist that humans had no memory of their first three years. Any memory we thought we had was planted by our parents. I don't believe this, but it does point toward some interesting possibilities. Certainly, I have few memories of that time. I think I have one: the sound of my parents' footsteps in snow as they pushed a closed-in sled that I lay in. They couldn't possibly have told me that memory because they wouldn't have known what I was hearing. Their memory could only be about what was observable to them.

Yet I could easily have created that memory out of the sled (which was used for years with my younger brothers and sisters), and out of later memories of the sound of footsteps in snow. There are many possible ways I could have shaped that story, that memory.

Is there an amnesia in our first years of existence, a process of forgetting a previous life? Is this a transit from life to life? Do we lose that old memory before we begin to remember again and build the next life? I have no beliefs here. Only an openness to possibility. Perhaps not all the memories of the previous life are forgotten, and they hook onto the memories I begin to make in my current life. You can see that this could take me anywhere.

Not long ago I heard a story of a two-year-old child dying. This girl's three-year-old brother was overheard asking his sister to remind him, once she was gone, what it was like where they came from because he was beginning to forget. Possibility.

But that's all, a possibility. I do not remember much of my past, perhaps nothing with accuracy. I don't know where I'm going. Meanwhile, though, I am constructing what I call "my life" out of memories, the memory of my senses, and the spiritual states these can lead to. I have no way of knowing if I have memory of anything other than what my senses give me, in this or other lives. Shifting memories. Memory construction. A weaving of apparent facts and what we need to do with the facts to create our lives. The facts themselves altering, modifying through time.

I can't see the beginning or the end of the river. Something nags at me. Longing. I experience, and express, this longing in poetry, in music. If I wanted to get into physics, or reincarnation, I'd have to say that I don't even know if my longing is for the past or for the future. Or if those two are the same. I just know the moment on the boat, and the motion. The motion itself is longing, and I write it and sing it. Otherwise I am exiled from memory.

As I'm sensually alive, the world presents itself to me in material terms first. All else seems to follow from that. So I love the things, the sounds and tastes and textures of the world. As I grow older, I value the physical world more. Quite possibly this is because I recognize, deeply, that I am losing that world. My eyesight grows clouded, my hearing goes, but, most importantly, my own death is something more than a concept of some distant future event. In my body I know I am nearing the mist ahead of me.

So much of the writing, the poems, that occupied me when I was a young man in love with ideas lose their resonance, and I find myself entering simple songs of longing. Songs for what is and what is not. Milosz, in his nineties, wrote:

> How ridiculous to deliberate on the aesthetics of Baudelaire
> amidst the crooked fences of a little town
> where hens rummage in the middle of a dusty street.

In the beautiful, hymn-like "Let Evening Come," Jane Kenyon wrote:

> Let dew collect on the hoe abandoned
> in the long grass.

And a Portuguese *fadista* sings:

> If you pass by the graveyard
> On the day of my burial
> Tell the earth not to eat
> The curls of my hair.

It's not that we remember events; we simply remember. What vanishes never was.

Limoncino Road

SITTING ON MY BALCONY SIPPING LIMONCINO and listening to music. Limoncino is an Italian lemon-based liqueur that pours lemon sun into your guts as you drink it. Doing that, this afternoon, under a blue sky in Vancouver. Almost the blue I grew up with in Manitoba. And I've got Big Dave McLean singing the blues on the CD player; the sound of Winnipeg, that raw, intense, straight-forward integrity. Lucília do Carmo comes on, too, with "Maria Madalena." *Saudade*: not so much longing for a physical home, in this song, but the condition of longing that is inherent to passion and sorrow.

Sometimes you have to get to the point of enough. That lemon shine inside that can go anywhere, and sometimes you have to go way past enough. Sometimes you just have to get out of yourself, however you do it without harming yourself and, more importantly, others. Sometimes, I suspect, you can't help but harm yourself before you get to where you're going. There's so much civilization, so much deception, to work your way through.

More than enough. That is the need of experience. Everyone's felt it; many have gone there for a while and returned, some didn't, others backed off, or put one foot in, testing the water. Going too far is dangerous, possibly physically but, more importantly, in other ways.

Beyond enough, and yet the poet needs to return from there and, knowing something about human beings and about craft, has to write a little less than enough. Just the right space or time between the two. Perhaps this is the crux of poetry. The poet has not only to leave, but create, room for the listener. There has to be a created space between the experience and the transmission of it. It can't be said like an equation. It's impossible, to begin with; language does not have that capacity. When someone tries to reproduce the experience, exactly, in language, you're left with bad writing.

The art is in writing less, in underwriting, but in underwriting with such skill that the listener will not only be able to fill the space but, more importantly, yearn to fill it. And, in filling that created space, the listener reaches his or her own experience beyond enough. This is the collaboration of poet and listener. How can anyone, unless they're easily sated by sentimentality, laugh or cry if everything is done for them? The held-back cry, that understanding, happens in that smallest of moments, of spaces, between the words and the experience.

Today I sip limoncino and live, briefly, in lemon fire. It can happen other ways, like writing out of late-night exhaustion. I get up and write some notes; phrases, thoughts, emerging that wouldn't have otherwise. The poem is rarely complete, and I know that. When I read the lines later, tomorrow, I may well see they are simply self-indulgent, excessive to a point beyond redemption. However, I may find it's all done or, more likely, there is something that holds within it the whole poem that has not yet been written. There's my work, to approximate the motion of my thinking of a few hours ago, or yesterday. Inevitably, it will find its own direction, possibly something quite different from what began.

By now I'm listening to another kind of music, *Spiegel im Spiegel*, by Arvo Pärt. Some of his writing agitates me in a way that does no good. But there are several sublime pieces, and this is one that speaks to that easy cliché of less is more, where some kind of excess is experienced, then reduced. The simplicity of the piano with the violin weaving in and out. I am given the gift of filling in the spaces where they need filling in, and leaving them where they need to be left. My heart is full, and my mind is quietly moving.

Great singers do the same thing. They chop the ending of a word, or they eliminate a word altogether. They pause within a line where other singers would not. The pause is held just long enough for you to want to fill it in, and perhaps you do. Perhaps you fill it just as the singer does and, at that moment, you and singer are one. You are singing the song, even if you are silent. Sometimes I think it's about the need, nothing else, the need for voice.

Patrick Friesen   127

Voice, however, has various connotations. Voice can be the sound you hear, but it is also, if you find it, the fundamental self. The self that is always there amongst the many selves we develop. The one self that all the other selves refer to, emerge from. The one self that is you on earth, and possibly beyond.

And, I suspect, one has to find a way beyond enough to find this self. Paradoxically, going outside oneself, the self created by civilization, to encounter self. And I may just be talking about the fire; I may be talking about my visits via specific poems, phrases I hear in conversations, songs, certain voices, the trembling of aspen leaves, water in its variations. This hot afternoon I'm talking about Via Limoncino.

Granada Water Songs

IN THE OLD PART OF GRANADA pretty well anywhere you stop and listen you will hear water. It might be the faint sound of the Darro River rustling in its narrow, shallow bed on the other side of the wall, or one of the innumerable fountains spouting; it could be a small rivulet of rainwater running down the centre of one of the alleys where the cobblestones dip to allow for runoff. There is water, and the music of water, everywhere.

If you travel up to the Alhambra, it becomes even more obvious. In the Generalife section of the Alhambra, the gardens, you walk from terrace to terrace, courtyard to courtyard. Everywhere are beautiful shrubs, flowers, trees, and everywhere are sources of water music. In one courtyard you hear six or seven spouts arcing water into stone channels; in another the channels are tilted so the water trickles down to the end and disappears into the earth. The next courtyard has a fountain at ankle height, with water burbling down the sides. Unless you stand absolutely still, even get to your knees, you probably won't hear this water. Or, you might run into a much taller fountain, where the water emerges at the top, spills over the side and drops into another basin, and from there to ground level. Water everywhere. And everywhere it makes different sounds. Some differences are obvious, some are utterly subtle.

For me, the most astonishing sight and sound is the water stair. This consists of about four or five flights of stone stairs with rounded stone banisters that have been halved and hollowed into runnels down which water flows. Walking up and down these steps you hear a dozen different water songs. Water running shallowly over a stone or, in a location where the banister has been carved into a slight circle, the water swirls about in a miniature whirlpool. It sounds different at the top where it begins its downward course from the bottom where it drops into a funnel. You walk up, or down, the stairs, and you become aware of the song, its shifting rhythms, its modulations.

As I walk away from the courtyards, I continue hearing water. At first I can't see it, but then I find it a few feet into the forest parallel with the path, gurgling along a stone run. I follow until it dips into the earth and disappears. I keep walking. After a hundred yards, the water re-emerges on the other side of the path and runs parallel to it for a ways. This keeps happening. I find rivulets, loud streams, tinkling fountains. No matter where I stand, I hear water.

And I think of Lorca. He used to come to Generalife and sit for hours looking at the gorgeous flowers, listening to the variations of water. It doesn't take much to find references to both in his poetry. The poem that comes to mind immediately is "Morning," where he refers to the harmonies of water, its cadences. He thinks of the song of water as a ballad singing beneath poplar trees.

He writes that "It is light made song. . . ." Christ, he says, should have told people that they could "Confess to the water / all your suffering, / all your shame." And he writes that "There is no condition more perfect / than when we drink water. / We become more childlike, / more good, and our cares pass. . . ."

This is an excess of water. Not as flood, but as the constant presence of its innumerable sounds mingling, playing off each other. One expert estimates Generalife has 1,000 different sounds of water. As I spend the afternoon drifting through terraces and courtyards, sitting sometimes in the shade, I am aware, perhaps, of forty different water sounds. That is enough to fill me. And, yet, I feel light. I feel motion in stillness. I am in an earthly paradise.

This doesn't seem to be the water of Gwendolyn MacEwen's poem "Water" in the *T. E. Lawrence Poems*, where water is not sound but, literally, life or death. In that poem, in that world, you walk "sparingly between wells." But the two poems are connected: it is the same water. For MacEwen "water is everything. . . . / It has / All tastes and moods imaginable / water is history. . . ." It is the scarcity of life-giving water in the Moorish deserts that had, undoubtedly, driven a sultan, some five or six hundred years ago, to divert river water eight kilometres to the Alhambra. Not as drinking water, but as dance, as the music that deeply quenches the soul's thirst. Water as physical necessity and as serenity.

I travel Lorca's last route, from his parents' summer house, the Huerta de San Vicente, in a park that used to be outside Granada but is now within city limits, to the Rosales house he hid in hopelessly, to the room in the civil government building where a Falangist thug had him imprisoned, up the road out of Granada into the foothills of the Sierra Nevada, through the town of Víznar, to a small building where he was kept for about five hours, and then further into the foothills, along a ravine to a bare spot beside the road, a spot that used to be filled with olive trees, but where only one now stands. There he was murdered. I'm told that in those years an old Arab aqueduct still ran near La Colonia, the house where Lorca was kept before execution. For the last hours of his life he heard water running, water which was so fundamentally important to him in his life and poetry. I see the ruins of this aqueduct near the spot where he was murdered. And, a little distance past that place, by Alfacar, is The Fountain of Tears, a former source of water for Granada, named before Lorca's execution.

Water everywhere, and its music. Its varieties of music. Weeping songs, old ballads, joyful outbursts. Voices of water. And I understand how water is fundamental to our humanity, not only our physical existence, but to our spiritual survival. We are born from water.

It sings in Granada, but it has its song on the prairies, where I grew up, as well. Different sounds, but still music. I remember how the air smelled before a rain, how it seemed to thicken, and then release as the rain arrived in a rushing downfall. I remember the sound of rain, in its variations of intensity, on the roof as my body eased into sleep. Or, waking slowly in the morning, the sun up, but drops of night rain still dripping leaf to leaf outside my window. After hundreds of thousands of years, the sound of water lives in my cells.

Poetry As Necessity

POETRY BEGAN EARLY. It began as a love of the sound of the human voice. I probably heard conversation first, but possibly I would have heard song first. Both my parents sang around the house. It was a religious household so many of the songs were hymns. However, my mother also loved singing Irish and Scottish ballads. She had a romantic connection with the ballads and tales of these two countries that probably began in the public school system. My parents' native language was a dialect known as Low German; in church, High German was often spoken.

So, I heard song early and, through my mother, I learned to read before I began attending school. She read to me, she sang, and she played the piano. So, for me, learning to speak (I learned both Low German and English at home; I studied High German in school), learning to read, and hearing songs and music, was all connected.

Quite early on I was also exposed to the rhetoric of sermons. While the ministers were elected from within the membership of the church, and the chance of getting a great speaker was minimal, there was still a style to sermons and an interweaving of sermon and reading of biblical text. The most common sermon was the talk based on one biblical text. Sometimes the sermon would interrelate several texts within the bible. Always, of course, making a moral point, or preaching doctrines. I grew to be repelled by doctrine and dogma, and by the misuse of language to promote it.

However, it seems to me, an exposure to this kind of analysis of text, not complex and driven primarily by the need to reinforce already-existing beliefs, promoted a perception that words are important, individually, and strung together. As a side comment on the importance of language, swearing was severely frowned on, but so was the use of imprecise or excessive language, so that if I was hungry and said I was "starving" my father would correct me with "people are starving in many parts of the world; you're not starving." One can see how this attention to text, to its intricate meanings, and to its power, could contribute both to the writing of poetry and the work of teaching.

When the sermon wasn't being preached, songs were sung. Sometimes trios or quartets sang from the stage, but most of the singing was congregational. So, music (when I was very young only singing was allowed in church, no instrumentation; however, instruments were played at home), song and words surrounded me. They didn't surround me in an everyday way of listening to one's Discman, hearing people talk. No, song and word were linked with religion and had significance. They were signs pointing toward a spiritual meaning.

I'd sometimes notice my mother writing poems on a Saturday night as she gazed out the window, watching snow fall. I didn't think much about what she was doing. It was just part of her life.

I remember loving the sound of the human voice whether in song or talk, and what I loved most was the sound of words. An interweaving of the texture of each individual voice and the sounds of words. I remember, when I was alone up a tree or lying on the grass, repeating specific words because the words sounded unusual. I remember two words off-hand. One was the word "stomach." I had seen this word in a book but had no idea what it was. I was a voracious, impatient reader so I'd just continue reading past the words I didn't know. Eventually, from context, I'd figure them out. That's what happend with "stomach." It suddenly clicked. What an odd spelling for that sound. Another word was "doldrums." I loved the sound of that word. What I think children do is take the external material world and internalize it as their own private thinking, their own mulling of language and song and image. This is also the space of the poet.

I was discovering language through its sounds and its pictures. I never stopped being fascinated by the sounds and pictures of language. To this day they seem almost miraculous. What a wonder that we can make marks on a page and read them silently and, fairly accurately, understand what someone has been thinking. A wonder that we use our lips and teeth, tongue, and other parts of the body, to emit sounds that listeners can understand reasonably well. Language as physical.

For me, language was a way of finding out about myself as a human spirit and body in a material world. It was a way of finding out about that physical world, about the possibility of spirit within the physical. Somewhere Joseph Brodsy said something about poetry being revelatory, not mimetic. Poetry does not imitate, it reveals. It opens up, lifts the leaf. It doesn't pronounce. It moves always, occasionally pausing on an image or sound, an almost frozen moment, then moves on. As the world does, as thinking does. Things associate with each other. Objects, emotions and thoughts, names, events. Poetry not only shows this happening, it takes part in the process. Poetry is rhythmical not only in the metrical sense, but in that it is the rhythms of thinking. That, at least, is the case for me. No established form seemed to suit me well. It took me years of writing, and reading aloud, to find the line length, the phrasing, that most suited my thinking. No one could teach me this.

Beyond the sound and image in words, I was attracted to the subtlety of connotative meaning. How wonderful that you could use the same word to mean different things. Sometimes this difference was dependent on the other words around that one word; other times it was dependent on how the human voice inflected the word, or paused just before it, or made some other shift in the voice.

There was a way in which one could communicate thinking and feeling without totally closing off the thought or feeling. There was an openness to poetry I didn't find as easily in most of my later reading of philosophy or theology. I was interested in ideas, but I disliked ideology. Ideology seemed like death. Poetry allowed me to explore my own thinking about experience, about books I read, music I heard, without shutting it down with some summing-up statement.

Before saying a few things about being a teacher, let me touch on something that may not seem obvious. Poets, generally, do not have the opportunity to practice poetry for a living in our society. With a very few exceptions, poets must work at other jobs or choose to live at the edge of poverty. This is a reflection of the kind of society we live in. It applies to varying degrees to all art forms. It is an odd thing that we make artists do things other than their art to make a living.

That said, I would say I'd be a teacher even if I could make a living as a poet. Not necessarily a teacher in any institution, but nevertheless a teacher. I believe this comes with the territory of being a poet. I learned from those before me, and I know I can offer my small piece in that continuum of poets and teachers of poetry. It would be informal, usually one-on-one wide-ranging talks; sometimes, specific editing of one or two poems.

Anna Akhmatova, the Russian poet, gathered about her, in her last years, four young poets. Joseph Brodsky was one of them; Anatoly Nayman was another. Sometimes they'd meet as a group, usually it would be one or two of them meeting with her at her dacha, or in one of the homes she stayed in, depending on whether she was in Moscow or Leningrad. Nayman has written a book about her in these circumstances. They talked about anything and everything. Politics, anthropology, music, current gossip in the arts community at large, and specific poems written by one of "Akhmatova's four orphans," as they called themselves, or by Akhmatova herself. She might, for example, quote a quatrain from Pushkin or Shakespeare and show how a couplet by Pasternak came out of that. She would make suggestions as to how they could improve poems, or tell them what worked. She also read poems of her own, and they would comment. Sometimes they would question a line, or verse. She might discuss it right then, or she might shift subjects but work on the problem verse later. Or not, if she thought they were wrong. It was understood she knew more about the craft than they did, she knew the history of Russian and world poetry better than they did, and she had had more experience in life than they had. So, they were there to learn from her, but she also learned from them. The learning was not formal; it could occur in various ways. It was intelligent, poetic conversation, wide-ranging and in-depth. They would exchange letters as well, go for walks amongthe trees. Sometimes they'd be very silent. Sometimes one of them would be working on a poem at the table while Akhmatova wrote a letter to someone else. A still room. Then, suddenly, a remark about something in the letter, perhaps. And maybe nothing further, or a conversation would emerge from this. They carried on their various conversations from time to time, through different mediums, threads in a tapestry.

This was, and is, teaching and learning at its best. An individual poet can develop an individual voice in such an environment. The difficulty with institutional creative writing is a tendency toward uniformity of voice (often the teacher's voice), of competence, but no voice based on experience, on individual experimentation and choices.

However, I live in this society, and I've always needed to work at other jobs. I drove a taxi, I worked in a factory, I taught junior high school for half a dozen years, I worked on a survey crew, I worked as a director of film, radio and video for Manitoba Education.

Over the last dozen years I have taught creative writing in Manitoba and British Columbia. I have also taught English literature at both high school and junior high school level and, very briefly, as a teaching assistant at a university. I do not consider myself an academic. Although I loved attending university, studying history and English literature, particularly, there came a day when I knew the theoretical language in my MA program was anti-poetry for me. I found it a way of seeing the poem that was quite different from how I experienced poetry. I could do the analysis, could understand the theories, but they were proving to be counter-productive to my own process as a poet. It felt a bit like doing an autopsy. I walked out. At the same time I need to say that I had two or three professors who were not performing autopsies, and they were immensely encouraging to me. I hold them in high regard.

I am a teacher of creative writing. I wonder about this job often. There were no creative writing courses available when I was at university. I learned by reading great writers, or writers I found close to me, by imitating them in order to learn, by trying variations on them. I took them apart, too, in my own way. Not in terms of meaning, but in terms of craft. How did they do what they did? And why did it work, or not? Those were the crucial questions, and this was the technical aspect of my apprenticeship. Living, with its many necessities, marrying, having children, holding a job, all these were my content, informed and shaped my content.

I don't believe I can make a poet out of anyone. At best, I can make better readers of people, or help someone discover they are a poet. I can teach craft, and I can use whatever knowledge I have, whatever experience I have, to create an environment of love of creating, of wanting to enter a creative process, of seeing the in-

136   *Interim: Essays & Mediations*

terrelatedness of all things on earth. I tell my students this. When a student asks me what next creative writing program he or she should take, I usually answer with "get a job, work at something, preferrably physical and hard." I encourage them to not get work within the literary business.

First off, that's a ghetto of poor pay and long hours. More importantly, it is an environment related to poetry, but it is not an environment that leads to using language elementally to explore and reveal experience, self in the world. In other words, enter life and live it at many levels. If you lock yourself into years and years of studying creative writing you tend to write incestuously. What experience do you write out of? Do you write out of a hothouse of theoretical discussions and arguments? Do you write only for other creative writing students, for your teachers? There are many poets who write very competent poetry. There are few that earn their own unique voices. This is a phenomenon that has been noticed by many, including editors of literary magazines in Europe. Creative Writing classes have flourished more in North America than in Europe. This has been a relatively recent flourishing; according to Karl Shapiro, beginning after World War II.

It becomes important to see such courses as places to learn craft and technique. To see such courses as goads for students to get out and live and write out of their living. In that way such courses can have value.

I am a teacher, not an academic. An old-fashioned teacher, probably. I learned from my teachers, teachers of English, of history, philosophy, and so on. I'd love to name some of them, but no one would know who they were. Several have died. They entered their classrooms with knowledge, humility, a desire to share their love of poetry, and open hearts. You can't do much better than that.

I find teaching very rewarding most days. There are, as in all work, bad days. Sometimes I'm off, sometimes the class is, or perhaps just one student, and that effects everything. Part of my work as a teacher is to shape the classroom environment when I sense resistance or exhaustion or any number of things that can potentially dull the class.

The good days find me riding the skytrain back to my apartment with a feeling of satisfaction that I have done my best at sharing not only knowledge but love of poetry. Also, many times, the class, something that has been said in it, has started a thinking process in me. An image, perhaps, an idea voiced in a unique way. And it runs through my mind as I travel home, ready to begin on my own work.

Equally, I usually enter class with some idea, an image, a phrase I love, something that has preoccupied me in the last few days. I don't hesitate to bring in the excitement of my own thinking process, my writing process. Or, I may have read that Milosz died, or Miriam Waddington. I bring in the obituary and read it, or I bring in a poem by the deceased poet. Not to study, not to take apart, just to read it. An honouring of one of my people, asking the students to understand these were human spirits on earth who chose poetry to leave some evidence behind.

Teaching and writing, for me, don't always have clear borders. They move in and out of each other. Why not? That's my life. Yes, teaching is a job, but it's more than that. It's one aspect of my life on earth, an important aspect. We all have had our teachers, and we all have, or will have, our students. It's a continuum. I hold within me the teachers who had an impact. I pass some of what they were on to my students. I often don't know I'm doing this. I do know, though, that one of the most important things I must do as a teacher is to let go of my students. We owe each other nothing but respect.

For me, the impact of my teachers was partly knowledge, but more importantly it was their commitment, their enthusiasm, and their complete openness to the poem. They taught me, not just by lecturing about it, but by entering it. At core, they knew the poem has a life, for a while. Everything passes away, including the best poems. Thinking changes, the imagination changes, language changes. But, if the poem has been well-written, has been absorbed by readers and, more importantly, by future poets, it will carry on in altered form. What I have absorbed from D. H. Lawrence or from Gwendolyn MacEwen may not show directly in my own poetry, but it still flows there. And so it lives in another way.

You have to love language, love poetry. You have to give yourself to your life. You have to accept dark and light. You have to be crazy; you have to enter it fully, without fear. This is not a career; it's a living.

A Simple Excursion

For Marijke, Niko, and Leigh

In July of 1973, a prairie storm passing over Winnipeg, I watched my daughter Marijke being born. I had not imagined the moment so muscular, so filled with her mother's hard work, so awesome. I had not imagined such a beautiful daughter. When I got home from the hospital, I found that hail had broken each window of our two-storey house. A gentle, cool breeze passed through the rooms. I wrote her name down on a pad of paper beside my typewriter, then fell asleep. When I woke, I looked through the name book on the table, but I couldn't find her name there. To this day I don't know where it came from. It was given.

Just an hour and a half past Christmas, in 1977, I rushed about boiling water, finding towels, to help a midwife deliver my son Niko. It was a home birth. He hadn't yet crowned, but the midwife told me the cord was wrapped around his throat. She cut it, saying he had to emerge in a minute or so, or he'd not make it. I shifted my attention to his mother, trying to help her in the hard work of birthing a child. Out of the corner of my eye I saw him slip out, then heard his first cry. He had made it; he would be a shyly smiling, quiet child as if he knew something none of us did.

Before both of these births, in May 1971, my mother and I held my father's hands as he died. I remember that I was breathing sympathetically with him without intention. Long, slow breaths. Then, suddenly, I realized that this present, single exhalation was a transition. He wouldn't inhale; I would. My body would insist on it. There was that moment where both of us were out of breath. The living and the dead. I took my breath. He gazed past us.

Three moments of wonder. The certainties of those moments and, in between, what we call our lives. While the births were amazing experiences, they weren't as astonishing as the death. I have a sense where the child comes from, how it was created, but I haven't any notion of where a human goes when the last breath is lost. Yes, there are explanations, scientific and religious, but in the face of it, I found myself bereft of knowing. All I knew was that this man, this familiar man, was gone, and I knew I would miss him the rest of my days. How can a being disappear absolutely? How can the physical realities of a voice, of hands, of a way of walking, vanish?

What I would miss was his life, its details. But I would be reminded of them now and then, usually in something I saw in myself, but later in what I saw in my children. Things go on, no matter what. There is the illusion of stasis, but everything keeps moving. I think of my father often. None of his grandchildren were born before his early death. When I, and my brothers and sisters die, all direct memory of him goes. We are not long for this earth. There will be stories for a while, stories based on memories, shifting and shaped, but in short time all will be forgotten.

Some die slow deaths, others die in a moment. Some die in bed, others in snow or water.

Everything keeps going. Grief turns to sorrow, sorrows lessen and move to a different place within us; we find the happiness, sometimes the joy, within our ordinary, civilized, habitual lives. We marvel at births and take delight. We love. We savour the moments when it feels we're outside of time, like the child. And, unexplainable as it may be, we continue.

Acknowledgements

Many thanks to Allan Safarik for his sharp-eyed, empathetic editing of this book.

And deep thanks, also, for ongoing reading and editing of my work, to Per Brask and Eve Joseph.

Some of these essays have appeared, sometimes in a slightly different form, in the following books and periodicals:

"I Could Have Been Born in Spain" in *Why I Am a Mennonite: Essays on Mennonite Identity*, edited by Harry Loewen, 1988;

"Haircut" in *Rhubarb Magazine*, 2005;

"Without a Bowtie" in *Prairie Fire*, Vol. 20, #1, 1999;

"Jugular Music" (Caroline Heath Lecture, 1996) in *Freelance*, November/December 1996;

"Poetry, Again" in *Second Chapter: The Canadian Writers Photography Project*, by Don Denton, 2004;

"How Like An Angel Came I Down!" in *Essays on Kushner's Angels*, edited by Per Brask, 1995;

"Poem as Sabotage," published as "Poets of the Russian Revolution," in *Brick Magazine*, Summer, 1992;

"Desire and Prayer" in *Trace: Prairie Writers on Writing*, edited by Birk Sproxton, 1986;

"A Handful of Water," as "Gathering Bones," in *Poetry and Knowing: Speculative Essays & Interviews*, edited by Tim Lilburn, 1995;

"Clearing" in *Event: The Douglas College Review*, Vol. 31, #1, 2002;

"The Dance Floor," as "Through the Curtain," in a program for a contemporary dance festival in Winnipeg, 1986;

"Snow in Trieste" in *Geist Magazine*, Summer, 2005;

"Memory River," forthcoming in an anthology to be published by Gaspereau Press, 2006; and

"The Dog Outside the Dream" and "Limoncino Road," forthcoming in the anthology, *Half in the Sun*, to be published by Ronsdale Press, 2006.

Works by Patrick Friesen

the lands i am
bluebottle
The Shunning
Unearthly Horses
Flicker and Hawk
You Don't Get To Be a Saint
Blasphemer's Wheel: Selected and New Poems
A Broken Bowl
St. Mary at Main
Carrying The Shadow
the breath you take from the lord
Bordello Poems

CDs

small rooms
Calling the Dog Home

Plays

The Shunning (adapted from the book)
The Raft

Poetry Translations
(from the Danish, in collaboration with Per Brask)

God's Blue Morris, by Niels Hav
The Woods, by Klaus Høeck
A Sudden Sky, by Ulrikka Gernes

Patrick Friesen has published twelve books of poetry and written two full-length stage plays, as well as several radio plays. A multi-genre author, he has collaborated with choreographers, dancers, musicians, and composers, and has released two CDs along with his numerous publications. In 1994 his book, *Blasphemer's Wheel*, won the McNally Robinson Book of the Year Award in Manitoba. His collection, *Broken Bowl*, was nominated for the Governor General's Award for poetry in 1997. His most recent book of poetry is *the breath you take from the lord*.